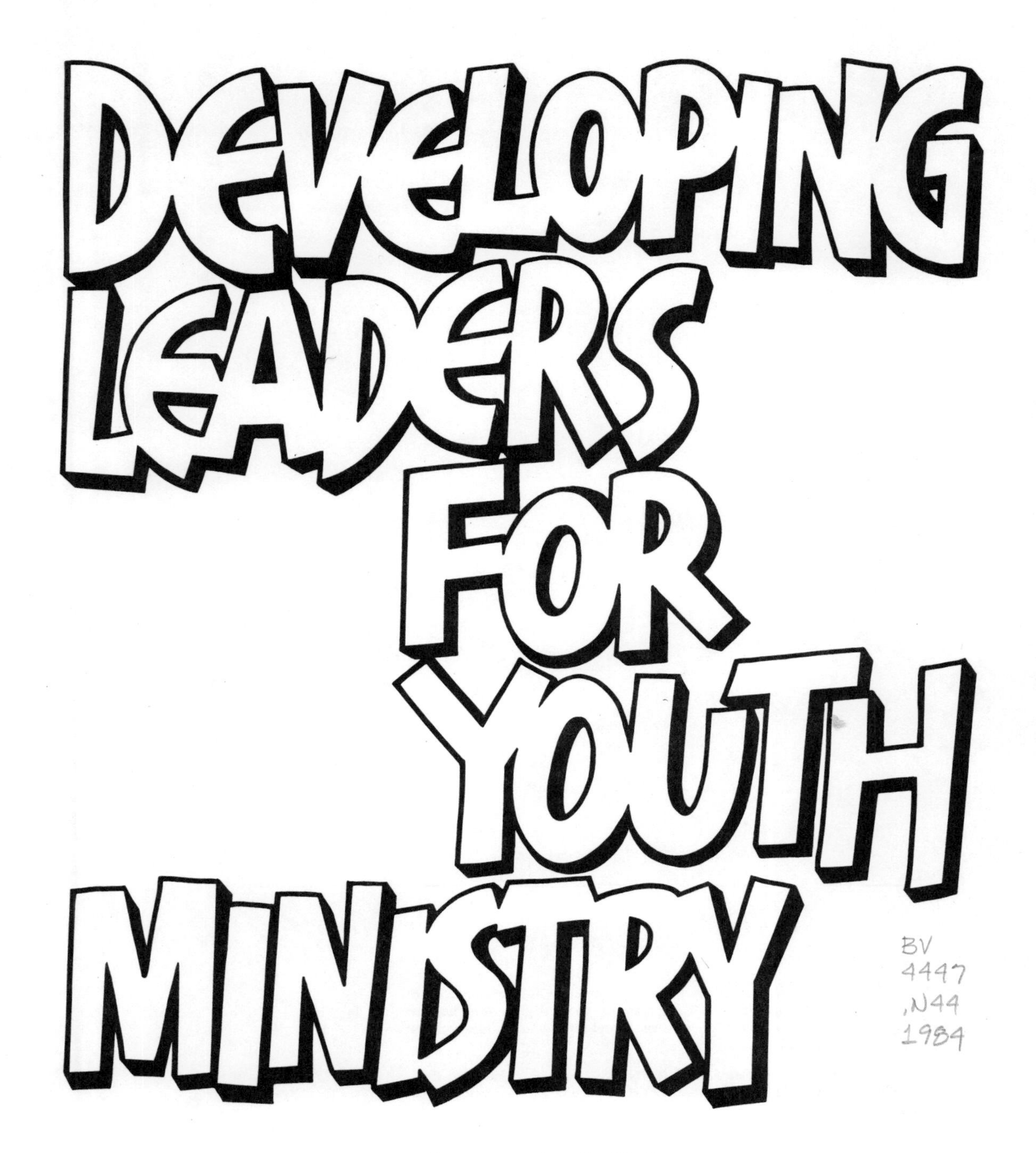

David Ng

Judson Press ® Valley Forge

DEVELOPING LEADERS FOR YOUTH MINISTRY

Library of Congress Cataloging in Publication Data

Ng, David.
Developing leaders for youth ministry.
Bibliography: p.
1. Church work with youth—Handbooks, manuals, etc.
I. Title.
BV4447.N44 1984 259'.2 84-7144
ISBN 0-8170-1032-7

Printed in the U.S.A.

Contents

Acknowledgments

Quotations from *Religious Education Ministry with Youth,* edited by D. Campbell Wyckoff and Don Richter, are used by permission of Religious Education Press, Birmingham, Alabama.

Funding for this project was received from the Lilly Endowment, Inc. Grateful acknowledgment is made to Robert W. Lynn for his guidance and help throughout.

The project was sponsored by Princeton Theological Seminary, to whom thanks are expressed for the many services provided throughout the work.

Participants in the Experimental Workshop

*Stephen F. Boehlke, Director, Alive, Ridgewood, New Jersey

William R. Forbes, St. Philip Presbyterian Church, Houston, Texas

*Freda Gardner, Associate Professor of Christian Education and Director of the School of Christian Education, Princeton Theological Seminary

Marlene LeFever, Administrative Editor/Special Projects, David C. Cook Publishing Company, Elgin, Illinois

David Ng, Associate General Secretary for the Division of Education and Ministry, National Council of the Churches of Christ in the U.S.A.

Jean B. Pinto, First Presbyterian Church, Pennington, New Jersey

Wayne Rice, Youth Specialties, El Cajon, California

*Don Richter, Second Presbyterian Church, Louisville, Kentucky

Manford Saunders, Executive Director, Willowbrook Ministries, Willowbrook Mall, Wayne, New Jersey

Robert W. Scott, Jr., United Methodist Church, Avalon, New Jersey

*Roger Uittenbogaard, Trinity Presbyterian Church, Cherry Hill, New Jersey

*D. Campbell Wyckoff, Professor of Christian Education, Emeritus, Princeton Theological Seminary

*Members of the Steering Committee

Foreword

This manual is one of the final products of a project sponsored by Princeton Theological Seminary and funded by the Lilly Endowment, Inc. A previous publication, *Religious Education Ministry with Youth*, edited by D. Campbell Wyckoff and Don Richter (Birmingham, Alabama: Religious Education Press, 1982) reported on the first phases of the project.

Our research has centered on the question "How may churches become recommitted to a vital ministry with youth?" In order to make available in handy form what is known about youth and youth ministry, Don Richter, director of the project, and then a student at Princeton Theological Seminary, prepared an analytical and critical bibliographical essay based on the twenty-six books that represent the most important research and practice in youth development and youth work. That essay was published as chapter 1, "A Bibliographical Survey of Youth and Youth Ministry," in *Religious Education Ministry with Youth*.

A study conference was held at Princeton Theological Seminary in June, 1980, at which scholars and youth workers met to consider a series of papers that dealt with essential elements in the future of youth ministry. The papers, as they were delivered, were subjected to a running analysis and critique. Both the papers and the commentary make up the remainder of *Religious Education Ministry with Youth*.

In the final sessions of the study conference a series of convictions about youth ministry emerged (see p. 15 of this manual). When pressed for priorities among these convictions, the participants arrived at the following:

> The goal is to help youth and persons in youth ministry gain insight into self and community in relation to church and culture, in tension with God's vision of community. This means:
>
> 1. Evaluating the cultural context; learning how to deal with the "givens" that we may not even recognize in our particular corner of society. Specifically, what is involved is gaining insight in depth on youth in particular churches and communities, through training in knowing and interpreting youth in their particular communities and cultures.
>
> 2. Identifying and articulating the biblical vision of community, in order to work out what is to be dealt with distinctively in church youth work—the New Testament base, the core concepts, the components of Christian community.
>
> 3. Recognizing and developing skills in dealing with attitudes and relationships.
>
> 4. "Responding to God's activity in the world by basing youth work in action for social justice. Dealing with the challenges of an unjust and demanding world order; struggling with how to integrate the social complexities of justice and liberation with our personal agenda for wholeness and self-fulfillment."[1]

Among the practical follow-up activities that were recommended was the following: "Bringing youth, lay leaders, and parents together in sharing-learning experiences—'energizing experiences of community.' "[2]

Out of this emerged the idea of an experimental workshop in which these matters would be used within a leadership training model for youth ministry. The idea was to have a variety of experienced youth leaders go through the process, and then work out from their experience with it a model that could be replicated and widely used for such training.

This manual is the result of that process. It builds on the previous steps in the project. The experimental "Workshop on Nurturing Leadership for Youth Minsitry'' was carefully planned by the Steering Committee in bimonthly meetings following the conference of June, 1980. Don Richter reports:

> The intent was to move from theory to practice, designing a process that would enable participants to focus on their own ministries rather than on learning new gimmicks or program ideas for next Sunday evening. The committee gave shape to the design proposal and selectively invited participants who would represent a variety of situations in their ministry with youth. Rather than calling on specialists to lead us through the process, members of the Steering Committee (assisted by Marlene LeFever) took responsibility for this leadership. The workshop participants assembled at the Krisheim Study Center in Philadelphia, July 6-9, 1981.
>
> The *Orientation* was an opportunity to become acquainted with one another and to share the history and the vision of our project with the participants. This was conducted by D. Campbell Wyckoff, who also led us in a study of Galatians 3:23-4:7. The remainder of the afternoon and the early part of the evening were spent in exploring *Relational Factors,* guided by Roger Uittenbogaard. The group was engaged in exploration of our individual stories as youth and now as adults working with youth. We graphed our personal and religious life histories, discussed significant adults from our youth, role-played various youth leader types, evaluated our skills at reflective listening, and lifted up points of conflict in our commitment of time to youth.
>
> Our second day was given to *Faith Values*, led by Stephen F. Boehlke. Each of us recalled a biblical story that affirmed for us the good news of our present ministry within the faith community. These stories were related to a personal story in ministry with youth that conveyed the good news of faith. From this we determined what our respective faith values are and which ones we would like to cultivate in our ministry. In the evening Marlene LeFever led us in an experience of mime, relating it to the areas of relationship and faith.
>
> The third day was devoted to understanding the *Life-Style Issues* that confronted us as young persons and continue to influence us now. Freda Gardner guided our reflection on the heroes and heroines of our youth, and the possessions and character traits we valued, those values which have changed for us and those which have remained or have been set aside, and a current life-style issue which is problematic in our ministries with youth. Marlene LeFever followed this up in the evening with tangram art, storytelling, and exploration of various ''mediums and languages'' each of us might use in presenting a life-style conflict to a youth group.
>
> The final day was a time of reflection upon our experiences with the workshop process. David Ng used Thomas Groome's ''Shared Christian Praxis'' to guide us through an evaluation and give attention to the forming of an experiential model that would make our workshop process easy to reproduce. Having done this, we joined together for an expressive hour of worship focused on ''God is joy . . . in right relationships . . . in discovering the values of our faith . . . and in shaping our lives as maturing Christians.''

From this, David Ng has written the present manual, embodying the experience (with some appropriate changes) in such a way as to make it widely useful for youth and youth leaders. I have had the privilege of editing the manuscript, including contributions from other members of the workshop.

Keeping in mind that we hoped to produce:

- An experiential model of learning that will be applicable for youth and adults from diverse backgrounds and settings,
- A process that can be replicated in a three-day period,
- A model that emphasizes the goals for those entering the process, that is, the goals for youth and adults engaged in ministry,

we have some qualms about putting it in a book. The Christian church did not start with a book, but with one person influencing another. Although it soon developed a book, at first it spread from person to person and from place to place by word of mouth. Our hope is that the publication of this manual will foster rather than stifle that word-of-mouth process and that it will have a real multiplying effect.

D. Campbell Wyckoff
Princeton Theological Seminary

[1]D. Campbell Wyckoff and Don Richter, editors, *Religious Education Ministry with Youth* (Birmingham: Religious Education Press, 1982), p. 244.

[2]*Ibid.*, p. 245.

Part I

Preparation

Chapter 1

About the Manual

This manual describes a workshop for youth leaders and youth, designed to enrich youth ministry in the churches by helping youth and their leaders to know themselves and their potential better, and to see their roles in youth ministry in terms of fostering the Christian life, faith values, and relational factors, while at the same time enhancing worship, Bible study, and personal expression. The workshop process is based on an exploration of the fundamental issues in youth ministry and an exploration of the key roles for leaders who work with young persons. The specific workshop processes are designed to help youth and their leaders to reflect on these issues and roles, and to discover how youth ministry may best be focused, supported, and guided.

Most adults sense that the church's ministry with youth is deeper and fuller than merely providing young people with a place to meet and enjoy wholesome activities under adult supervision. At heart, youth ministry is persons in relationship. Young people and adults in a youth program become co-members of a caring-covenanting community. They are, together, a part of *the church.* In this caring-covenanting community adults serve as guarantors—role models—of the Christian life and community.

The role of "guarantor" is stressed because it implies personal support, leadership, and guidance in a friendly, understanding, and faithful relationship. The patterns of life and relationship practiced by adults (and leaders among youth) are examples and encouragements to junior and senior high school young persons during their time of identity formation and decisions about faith and values. The type of leadership offered by these adults and older youth who are guarantors is gentle—guarantors may be older and more experienced than the youth, and perhaps they may even be wiser or better trained—but they are partners with youth. Guarantors, partners, fellow pilgrims—these roles describe the adult and youth leaders in youth ministry. Young persons are on a faith pilgrimage, a journey through many experiences of questions, prayer, service, recreation, study, reflection, and decisions. Those who are chosen as leaders in youth ministry have the privilege of being fellow pilgrims journeying with the young persons, exploring, guiding, and discovering with them in the youth ministry pilgrimage.

Yet another key role for leaders is that of disciple. Leaders are persons who follow Jesus Christ and who call young persons to a common commitment to Christ and the Christian life.

To "get at" the concerns described above, this manual describes a workshop with these purposes:

- To identify several key roles for leaders who work with youth.
- To gain a vision of youth and adults in a community of faith in which each person contributes unique gifts of faith and ministry.
- To gain some insight into how young persons experience spiritual formation.
- To become aware of what it means to live as the people of God in a particular cultural setting.
- To begin to perceive and respond to biblical mandates for justice and servanthood.

The Workshop—For Whom?

This workshop experience is intended to serve youth and adults who are leaders or potential leaders in youth ministry. This includes:

- Youth who are leaders in youth ministry programs
- All adults who work with young persons
- Assigned leaders

- Youth ministry administrators
- Christian education administrators
- Pastors
- Support personnel (for example, the people who look after the financial affairs of youth ministry, the buildings and equipment, and who take care of things such as food and recreation)
- Other interested and concerned adults:
  - Potential leaders
  - Parents
  - Christian education committee members
  - Church governing council members

The audience includes both beginners and experienced workers in youth ministry. Certainly beginners appreciate all the help they can get, and they want to learn the basic goals and foundations of the church's ministry with youth. This workshop deals with such topics, which may be taken for granted and overlooked by more experienced workers with youth. There are many adults with years of experience who have not been given a chance to go beyond the roles of recreation leaders and program planners for youth; this workshop strives to reach beyond these topics to some deeper purposes of youth ministry.

Both volunteers and professionals are included. While it was professionals from a wide range of experience and work in the church and with youth who tested the workshop model, uppermost in their minds were the volunteers who make youth ministry possible. This workshop plan welcomes both professionals and volunteers, and challenges both.

The workshop is also suitable for a great variety of groupings. Here are some of the most obvious:

- Various groups in the parish (youth leaders, parents,

teachers, and youth themselves)
- Clusters of youth leaders in the community (youth leaders from the different churches, denominational or interdenominational, in a particular town or district)
- Groups in retreat centers
- Seminaries and colleges
- Continuing education seminars

There are other possible participants and groups, but this list will serve to indicate the wide spread of persons and groupings that those who designed the workshop model had in mind.

They also had in mind a wide variety of churches. The workshop is not designed with any one type in mind, but the emphasis is probably on the church of two hundred members or less—and the bulk of youth ministry takes place in such churches.

Elements and Emphases

The workshop experience involves three elements and three emphases, all of which will be developed in detail in the section on "The Design of the Workshop," and in other appropriate sections of the manual.

The elements consist of experiences that flow through every activity of youth ministry and that give it its basic character. They are:

- Worship

- Bible study

- Personal expression

The emphases are those aspects of youth ministry that the designers felt needed to be lifted up for concentrated exploration. They are:

- Youth ministry and the Christian life

- Faith values in youth ministry

- Relational factors in youth ministry

In the section on "The Design of the Workshop" practical matters of planning, securing, and orienting participants are discussed. Then each of the three elements and each of the three emphases is explained.

In a word picture of the workshop in action, six sections of the manual show:

How to Get Started (from getting acquainted and getting oriented, to the first Bible study)
Youth Ministry and the Christian Life (including explanatory material and a full description of the workshop activities)
Faith Values in Youth Ministry (activities designed to help youth and youth leaders to see and develop their own faith, and to consider how others may be helped to do so)
Relational Factors in Youth Ministry (activities showing how to deepen our relationships with God and with other people, focusing particularly on the relational responsibilities of leaders in youth ministry)
Pulling It Together (showing how the elements and emphases interplay and ultimately belong together; also showing how each participant in the workshop may "pull it together" meaningfully)
Following It Up (The workshop is intended to have a multiplying effect in which youth ministry programs continue to be enriched, and in which new persons are brought into similar workshop experiences.)

Various Uses of the Manual

Those responsible for designing the experimental workshop and carrying it through had in mind that they were setting in motion an enterprise that would serve a wide variety of uses, some of which were:

- To develop the youth ministry team.
- To develop potential leaders.
- To help Christian education administrators and decision-makers develop a philosophy of and approaches to youth ministry.
- To help parents and other adults understand the needs of young persons.
- To be adapted for use with young persons for their understanding of themselves.
- To train seminary students and other church workers.
- To serve as an example of a workshop method for training leaders, with more emphasis on issues than on techniques.

Chapter 2

The Design of the Workshop

The process of designing the workshop has to begin with setting a goal and recognizing the assumptions involved. In a general but useful way the goal of the workshop is:

> To encourage persons engaged in youth ministry to develop a more critical perspective on self and community in order to realize the redemptive possibilities and responsibilities that God calls us to claim in any given context of ministry with youth.

There is an immediate urgency to become more specific about the purposes of the workshop, and that is to be done when we get to the point of setting objectives. At this point the larger and more general goal is what we need to provide focus for designing the experience.

In order further to focus and understand the workshop experience, there are assumptions in our thinking that have to be recognized and voiced, for if they are left unrecognized and unspoken, we may soon find that we are planning at cross purposes. Those who designed the experimental workshop saw these five assumptions underlying their planning:

- Each person, youth and adult, has gifts for ministry. Effective ministry is a shared ministry of the community of faith.
- There is a need in youth ministry for a better understanding of the process of spiritual formation, how a youth is shaped in Christ.
- There are ways to increase our awareness of what it means to live as the people of God in a particular cultural milieu.
- Youth and adults, laypersons and professionals, are to be more fully integrated in nurturing leadership for youth ministry.
- The norms for effective youth ministry will be determined by our response to such biblical mandates as justice and servanthood.

Planning

Start with a nucleus of interested and concerned persons. Or start with just one concerned person! Find those who have the enthusiasm and persistence that is needed to bring the workshop to reality and to a successful conclusion. These people constitute the planning and steering committee.

Basic Issues

Agree on the basic youth ministry issues to be dealt with. At the 1980 Consultation on Youth Ministry, held at Princeton Theological Seminary, several days of intensive work produced this list of thirteen basic issues in youth ministry.[1]

1. Youth ministry must recognize its cultural context.
2. It is important to have a community that spans all ages in the church and that includes youth in the total life of the church.
3. We must learn to recognize and deal with conflicting expectations for youth ministry in the different segments of the congregation: youth, parents, clergy, lay advisors, the Lord (and the gospel mandate).
4. We must become familiar with support services, resources, and resource persons for youth ministry.
5. Youth ministry needs informed, "authentic" youth

[1] D. Campbell Wyckoff and Don Richter, editors, *Religious Education Ministry with Youth* (Birmingham: Religious Education Press, 1982), pp. 243-244.

leaders *and* other adults in the congregation who are willing to share their excitement about God's activity in the world and who are sensitive to the teachable moments.

6. The church must be open and alert to God's present activity in the world and to its mission in light of present converging crises.
7. Youth ministry must discriminate between Christianity and other faith commitments.
8. We must acknowledge the tension which exists between the church as a cultural construct and the church as a people of God.
9. Youth ministry cannot be confined to a narrow set of stereotypes about who best does ministry, nor only to certain expressions of faith or images of the church.
10. There is a need for front-line pragmatics, basic training, the gathering of practical models. For example, we should find out how effective youth ministers are spending their time.
11. We can identify guidelines for youth ministry based on the New Testament *koinonia* and provide room for local autonomy within those guidelines.
12. We should enable youth leaders to realize what they have to give to young people so that they will have the confidence to do it.
13. Youth ministry involves youth in mission.

Add to these basic issues. Then sort them out, and narrow them down to the issues that you need to face in your workshop. When the consultation did this, those in attendance identified four basic issues which they considered essential for the churches to resolve in the interests of the future of youth ministry.

Members of the planning and steering committee, the nucleus of concerned persons, will gain in their own understanding of the purposes of youth ministry, and will sharpen their focus for the workshop by engaging in discussions that lead to a consensus about the major issues or topics to present in a workshop. Equally helpful is consensus on which topics are secondary or even irrelevant to the goals of the church and its ministry with young persons.

Objectives

In line with the basic goal, the assumptions in the minds of the planners, and the issues that have been selected to be dealt with, more specific objectives begin to emerge. Those who planned this manual felt that specific objectives such as the following were likely to clarify and direct the workshop:

1. To help leaders on the youth ministry team to recognize three major areas in youth ministry: relational factors, faith values, and the Christian life—within a context of worship, Bible study, and personal expression.
2. To use a workshop process for examining these issues so that participants may experience aspects of the issues in personal and corporate ways.
3. To help identify key roles for leaders in youth ministry.
4. To strengthen the youth ministry team.
5. To foster individual growth in self-understanding and in youth ministry skills.

Go over these objectives carefully, and revise them to suit your particular purposes and to communicate accurately with those who will be asked to participate.

Build In Essential Factors

Certain factors are in the back of the minds of the planners. Get those factors out on the table, decide how important they are, and see that the important ones get built into the design. For instance:

Worship and Bible study will be the central, integrating dynamic.

There will be a balance of concern for the self and social issues. What is the method for a constructive self-understanding that can be presented to youth by committed adults? How do we learn to perceive the critical issues in a particular community?

The basic movements of the design process will be:
Lead,
Listen,
Dialogue,
Build.

Matters that will be considered throughout the process are:

- A theological critique of existing models and approaches in ministry with youth
- The institutionalization of youth ministry, both the benefits and the drawbacks
- The position of the youth minister, the title "youth minister," the single person in the ministry, the adult leader of youth as adult

Provide for Leadership

Recognizing that the planning group, the steering committee, is active in leadership throughout, select and recruit additional leaders as follows:

- A *convener* is needed to:
  Guide the process.
  Lead in analyzing the process as it develops.
  Lead in critiquing it as it develops.
  Lead in identifying its emerging creativities.
  Guide the summarization.
- A person will be designated to *observe* and *review* the work, giving help at strategic points and assisting with evaluation and future planning.
- Six persons are needed to take special responsibility for leading the group through the various dimensions of the educational experience, as follows:
  Planning and leading worship.
  Planning for and leading designated periods of Bible study.
  Planning and leading the group in activities designed for personal and creative expression (including dance, mime, music, and the like).
  Planning and guiding the section on "Youth Ministry and the Christian Life."
  Planning and guiding the section on "Faith Values in Youth Ministry."
  Planning and guiding the section on "Relational Factors in Youth Ministry."

Clearly, having been in on all the planning, members of the steering committee may be the persons best equipped to take on some of these responsibilities. They also have responsibility for seeing to all the arrangements and for seeing that things go smoothly.

Selecting and Inviting Participants

Review the kinds of people who should be invited to participate, and develop a roster of the names of persons who ought to be there. Who is there among the appropriate categories who ought to be invited?

- Youth who are leaders in youth ministry programs
- All adults who work with young people:
  Assigned leaders
  Youth ministry administrators
  Christian education administrators
  Pastors
  Support personnel
- Other interested and concerned adults:
  Potential leaders
  Parents
  Christian education committee members
  Church governing council members
- Both beginning and experienced persons in youth ministry.
- Both volunteers and professionals in youth ministry.

Consider carefully whether this ought to be a parish affair, whether it ought to include persons from other parishes of your denomination, or whether it ought to be interdenominational for the community or the region. Make your list of invitees accordingly.

If your plan goes beyond your own parish, be sure to try to include persons from more than one type of church. Remember that most youth ministry takes place in churches of two hundred members or less.

Take the setting into account in deciding whom to invite. Does the fact that it will be held in your own parish church, in a neighboring church, in a retreat center, at a seminary or college, in a continuing education center, suggest other possible participants to you? Going beyond your own congregation adds not only numbers of participants but also richness of questions and possibilities.

In selecting participants, there are certain criteria that are to be kept in mind. Persons with the following characteristics will be helpful:

Experienced or interested in youth ministry
Focused on *ministry*, with a special program as illustrative and supportive of this focus
Intentional
Dialogical—able to share self with others and vice versa
Constructive—building on the findings of our Steering Committee; helping us to test our hypotheses and generate new ones

Once you have determined the audience, devise a method of personal invitation. Whether it be individual letters, telephone calls, or conversations, personal invitations to the workshop convey its urgency, its goals and its style. A potential participant will gain from the invitation an impression that he or she is being asked to come to an important, well-planned event that demonstrates how leaders may communicate concerns of the church and serve the needs of youth.

Be Flexible

The ideas and specific suggestions given here provide a basic framework. They can be springboards for the planning group's own leaps of faith. The unique audience and local situation require the planners to adapt any printed suggestions for local use. As the planners strive for relevancy they may well obtain "ownership" of the plan—it will be a creation they have made and will carry out enthusiastically. Such enthusiasm and optimism can be conveyed to the participants.

Once the plans are made, inform the entire church or churches of the event and the hopes for it. The type of youth ministry that is advocated on these pages works best in the context of congregations that care for their youth and see the youth program as a part of the entire church's communal life. This attitude is fostered when youth workers take care to interpret to the congregation a holistic understanding of specific programs in the church.

Arrangements

Pay attention to arrangements, supplies, and equipment. A workshop is undergirded by attention to detail. Facilities that are conducive to group sharing must be found. It may be possible to obtain a retreat center or a neighboring church with comfortable, spacious meeting rooms and cooking and eating facilities. Almost as important as the adequacy of the main meeting room—with good seating, wall space for posting newsprint charts, etc.—is the space for activities that "just happen."

Conversations during breaks and free time, while lounging in easy chairs or sitting on the porch steps, are opportunities for the participants to review or test their learnings and to reinforce their partnership in youth ministry. What can be modeled in these casual times are informal listening and talking that are useful activities in actual youth ministry settings.

Many other details need attention. Transportation, supplies, equipment, and food or snacks may need to be obtained. Again there can be awareness of the "human and social values" of such ordinary details. While relationship and learning cannot be forced, workshop planners can still be mindful that traveling together, cooking and eating, and engaging in informal conversations are potential means of creating teamwork and reinforcing learnings about corporate Christian life.

Scheduling

Devise a workshop schedule. Such a schedule need not be printed in quantity if the planners prefer to convey a flexible, relaxed program. However, the planners themselves need a schedule as a guide and as an approximation of the time required for various activities. If three major areas or issues are dealt with, the workshop, of course, is structured around three blocks of time. For example, three blocks of four hours each (including time for breaks) may be set for each topic. Or a workshop can be built around six two-hour sessions, over a period of six weeks—each topic being dealt with in two sessions.

One of the most effective ways of conducting a workshop is in a weekend retreat setting. A weekend workshop at a nearby place might be scheduled in this manner:

Friday	5:00	Travel as a group.
	6:30	Soup and sandwiches. Bible study.
	7:45	Orientation and introductions.
	8:45	"Youth Ministry and the Christian Life."
	9:45	Snack and relaxing.
Saturday	8:00	Simple breakfast. Bible reading at table.
	9:00	"Youth Ministry and the Christian Life" (continued).
	12:00	Lunch.
	1:15	"Faith Values in Youth Ministry."
	4:30	Free time.
	6:00	Dinner.
	7:30	"Faith Values in Youth Ministry" (continued).
	9:00	Snack and relaxing.
Sunday	8:00	Simple breakfast. Bible reading at table.
	9:00	"Relational Factors in Youth Ministry."
	1:00	Lunch and closing worship.
	2:00	Return home.

"Adequate preparation is being a good steward of other people's time."

The Three Elements: Worship, Bible Study, Personal Expression

Throughout the workshop, three elements are built in as experiences that flow in and out in every segment: worship, Bible study, and personal creative expression.

Worship

Worship takes place at a number of points in the workshop schedule:

Around the meal table

In connection with each of the workshop's major emphases

After lunch, at the close of the workshop

These are times of public, group worship. There will also be private worship—some spontaneous and unscheduled, and some determined by the regular devotional practices of the participants. It is conceivable that occasions may arise in the midst of other activities for spontaneous and unscheduled group worship as well.

Why is worship so important in the workshop experience? One of our convictions is that relationships hold the key to youth ministry—and we do not mean only the relationship of youth to youth, or of youth to adults. Youth ministry depends also on divine-human relationships that are fostered by worship. In worship the individual engages in the most profound dialogue with God, a dialogue that is searching, revealing, judging, redemptive, and sustaining. In worship the individual joins with others in the same sort of dialogue, so that the experience gains a significant social dimension. Furthermore, worship is a service that we render to God in adoration and commitment. In that relationship we are transformed—we grow, change, and are renewed.

In planning for the worship experiences in the workshop, consider both traditional and innovative elements. The liturgies may sometimes be formal, sometimes informal and spontaneous. The music may include both the great hymns of the church and more modern songs. Whatever modes are used, however, plan them dialogically and expectantly.

Bible Study

The Bible is basic for the church. The community of faith constantly seeks God's message as it listens to the Bible read and interpreted in worship, in small groups in the church, and in individual study and reflection.

There is today a great need for positive modeling of Bible study. Both leaders and young persons need to participate in it, to see and hear it done. A workshop on how to do youth ministry may be a setting for teaching members of the community of faith how to be the church in search of God's Word.

Bible study in a retreat setting may be part of table fellowship as the group shares a meal and then moves simply and naturally into a time of sharing in Bible study. At the end of a meal after the table is cleared, the group studies an appropriate Bible passage.

Take Ephesians 4:7, 11-16, for example:

- Have someone read the passage aloud, with the others following the reading in their own Bibles. (Or copies of the passage may be duplicated on sheets of paper with the discussion questions listed and with wide margins for notes.)
- A brief discussion flows from these questions:
  What may the author have been trying to say to the Ephesians?
  What does the passage say to you personally, right now?
  What does this passage say to us as a group? (Pursue what it says to us as leaders in youth ministry. What does it say about our task as leaders? About young persons? About the resources available to us for youth ministry?)
- As a final question, ask: "How do you hear God speaking God's Word to us in this passage?"

Suggestions for Bible study are made at a number of points in the workshop plan. As you use them, reflect on the passages that are chosen, and on the ways in which they are analyzed, discussed, and integrated into the workshop experience.

At some point in the process when you are fairly well into the workshop, stop and talk about how the Bible study fits into youth ministry, the ways it may be pursued, and what difference it makes to the individual, the group, and the church. Share experiences on how Bible study becomes meaningful to both youth and adults. How does one grow in one's ability to hear God speak the Word? What may one expect during the youth years? What may one expect during maturity?

Personal Expression

The dimension of personal expression in the workshop encourages the participants to communicate creatively and imaginatively with one another. It expresses what we are discovering about ourselves as we affirm our uniqueness in ministry.

Rather than being limited to one single block of time, personal expression is best integrated throughout the whole workshop. It may be the integrating dynamic of the workshop. As such, it is not explored as one segment of the program but is returned to over and over again. The overall task is to explore how we articulate and express meaning, however tentatively this may be done. What mediums are used and what language is employed for doing this? Can we begin to see an artistic wholeness or gestalt in our life pattern? At the end of the process we may be able to discern what "mediums and languages" have been effective in our lives and ministries. There may come an "Aha!" experience in claiming both our capabilities and our limitations in self-expression.

Personal expression may grow and develop as our experience together grows and develops, so that a great deal of it may be generated spontaneously during the workshop itself. The designated leader is not expected to do everything personally, but to draw on the many talents of the other participants in the workshop.

There will be youth and adults who may not really know each other, but who have at least three levels of concern:

Their own ministry with youth
Assistance to other leaders of youth ministry
The challenge to forge a model of youth ministry

These youth and adults already have "mediums and languages" for saying who they are and what their ministry is, and they may be invited to share them with the group. (One of the people invited to the experimental workshop happened to be extremely talented in creative dance, and was a marvel at helping others share that experience.) At the same time this will be a time for discovering new "mediums and languages" and trying them out. Such an experience in growth in mediums of expression and skill in using them can help to put life and faith together.

How does the community of faith express itself symbolically in the areas of repentance, prayer, and service? More is involved than ordinary role-playing or making a person feel accepted by the group. The closing worship, for instance, may become one of the chief points at which the group is "gathered" in a deep sense, where we use our "mediums and languages" expressively in relationship to God, ourselves, and our ministry.

The emphasis is not exclusively or primarily on our personal concerns, but includes those concerns that relate specifically to ministry with youth. The designated leader senses a concern emerging and plans a creative way to bring it to the fore. It is a matter of working in such a way that experiences dealing with expressive needs reflect the other areas—reflection on Bible stories and images, important people in our lives, values identification, tension and stress points as we work at youth ministry, reflection and projection in terms of ourselves, other adults, and youth.

As life-style issues, faith values, and relational factors are studied, the designated leader may pick up experiences, motifs, themes, and "mediums and languages" that may be reflected through personal expression. Since expression is more than self-discovery, reflection will reveal things to us that transcend ourselves and our situation. Choice of personal life-style expresses how we respond in our social context. Worship expresses what we are learning about the revelation of God's will to us (faith values). Communication expresses how we relate to other individuals and groups (relational factors).

Affirming our uniqueness in ministry inevitably gives rise to conflicts. A key factor for us is learning how to define the conflict and deal with it creatively rather than viewing it as schismatic or destructive. The expression of how faith values impinge upon and affect one's life-style is relational and is at base a creative conflict.

Personal expression is important both for young persons and for adult leaders. Adolescents need healthy, safe ways to articulate their inner feelings and moods and to raise questions about themselves, relationships, and faith values. Leaders need to express support and their own values in ways that are helpful but not overpowering. Since so much of youth ministry is expressed through personal relationships, the skills of encouraging personal expression are vital to the leaders' ministry with youth.

A nonthreatening atmosphere contributes to wholesome personal expression. Such an atmosphere is akin to that found in a home where there is acceptance of one another and freedom to be informal and expressive, so that feelings can be shown and thoughts can be spoken *and heard*. When leaders work with groups, they should try to create a similar atmosphere. To do so requires a sensitivity to expectations, inclusion, acceptance, and mutual responsibility.

The earlier material in this workshop plan urged good preparation. It was stressed that even before an event begins, people must be helped with their expectations. People need to know ahead of time not only what to bring and what to wear but, more important, what the goals and hopes for the event are, the types of behavior that will be appropriate, and the style of interaction that will characterize the time together.

The plans for the workshop call for the work of "inclusion." This useful word points to the necessity of activities early in an event (or even a simple meeting) to allow each participant to feel acceptance, to gain "ownership" of the agenda, and to have a sense of what the group is and how it intends to behave. In a workshop as well as in most youth programs, it is valuable to have some form of introduction and orientation, whether these are simple or complex, formal or informal. Until a person feels that she or he belongs, that person will not be comfortable in participating.

A participant who feels accepted can move on to a sense of mutual responsibility. Ideally, individuals in the group feel that they are present not only to gain information and skills for themselves, but also to contribute to the welfare of others. One's contributions are not mere recitations of knowledge to prove to a leader that one is paying attention. What one says is offered as a way to be mutual—to contribute to a common learning experience where people teach one another. A partial, untested answer is not considered to be an incorrect response, but to be a building block upon which the group can construct an understanding of the whole. Such a nonthreatening atmosphere can enhance personal expression and participation.

The Bible study at the meal table is an example of a simple attempt to allow for personal expression. In this case a basic structure of questions is used. The questions get at some substance by enabling personal expression in nonthreatening ways.

The several activities designed to introduce persons to one another have their creative sides and can set the tone for the free give-and-take of personal expression: asking persons to relate how they felt about the church when they were younger, role-playing, reflecting listening skills, and presenting a case study of a present conflict concerning youth and how we as a group can deal with it.

In a number of the study sessions, simple charts or lists of questions are provided for the participants. Individual work on these handouts allows persons to do private work without fear of having to show others the degree of their knowledge or the intensity of their feelings. In the follow-up discussions the participants are assured that they are to share only what they wish to share and they have the safety of silence should they so choose.

In worship we explore ways that are helpful in listening and being receptive to the Holy Spirit. We express faith values in modern stories and parables. We may compose new lyrics to a familiar hymn. (Note the use of storytelling, both in retelling Bible stories and in telling personal anecdotes and stories. The story is as old as humankind, but we are finding renewed powers of articulation from this basic form of human expression.)

Music provides not just a traditional form of creative expression, but an infinitely varied means for expressing new ideas, deeply experienced feelings, and partially realized yearnings. The use of music composed or performed by others serves often to stir thought and feeling that enable us to transcend who we are and who we have been.

In dealing with life-style issues, profound feelings may surface. Their expression, while sometimes presenting immediate difficulties in a group setting, may lead to relational gains and to theological reflection. Later the group may return to the issue to discern changes that have taken place.

The same values of personal expression are invited in the process of evaluation. What has been useful—unnecessary—constructive—threatening—gripping?

Many other forms of personal expression may be used in the workshop. Workshop planners and leaders of youth programs may wish to consult resource books for descriptions of interesting, practical, and nonthreatening forms of expression. Consider the use of role play, tangrams, cinquain poetry, pictures, cartoons without captions, coats of arms to be filled in, posters, bumper stickers, and graffiti boards. The list is endless.

If you are the designated leader in this area, come with a range of possibilities (a dozen? twenty?) that you can use as appropriate. Some you will use, some not. Others will appear as you go along. At some point you might say, "Here are some of the other things we might have done. I chose not to do them because. . . ."

The Three Emphases: The Christian Life, Faith Values, Relational Factors

The segments of the workshop that are given scheduled emphasis represent the three matters that appear to present youth ministry's greatest promise, and that require personal exploration in depth by those who are chosen as youth ministry leaders. The particular emphasis that is given to each one in this workshop is as follows:

Life-style issues—Engagement in the exploration of the demands upon us and the possibilities for us, both personal and communal, as God's people in this world.

Faith values—Direction in learning how to discover or rediscover for ourselves the biblical vision of redemptive possibilities and responsibilities, whatever the "givens" may be in our own lives and in those with whom we minister.

Relational factors—Guided personal reflection encouraging a new awareness of one's own youth, the relationship of one's personal needs to ministry, and the dynamics which one's personality brings to a given context of ministry.

Youth Ministry and the Christian life

In exploring youth ministry and the Christian life, there are four components to be considered. The first is self-reflection on the values and life-styles that commanded attention in the teen years, the values that we affirmed and incorporated into our lives in the adult years together with their continuities and discontinuities, and the barriers and deterrents that we can detect in the process of working on their incorporation.

The second is Bible study, and exploration and identification of biblical images and imperatives related to life-style characteristics.

The third is analysis and appraisal, in which we try to identify the range of possible expressions (the range of life-styles) that will embody those biblical images and imperatives, and in which we try to identify the tension points in the community in which a diversity of life-styles is present.

The fourth is implications for youth ministry: recognition of our own personal capacities and problems in relation to values and life-styles in ministry to and with youth, implications for leadership development, strategies for leadership development, and implications for life and ministry (including program for youth in the church).

The discipline of Christian service follows the discipline of repentance and prayer. Repentance is "letting go" of our idols and of our need to control everything.[2] This is the appropriate dynamic for life-style issues. As we examine the way society and Caesar have shaped our values and presented us with ethical dilemmas, we begin the process of letting go in a mutually supportive environment. Repentance is the worship dynamic involved in examining our lives in tension with God's expectations.

Faith Values in Youth Ministry

After we let go of our need to control, we are ready to "pay attention" to what God would have us do in the world. Prayer is the discipline of paying attention.[3] It is the appropriate worship dynamic for the area of faith values. The better acquainted we are with God's story in relation to our own stories, the better able we are to open our eyes and ears to the parables we live from day to day. Only after repentance and prayer are we equipped for the ministry of Christian servanthood.

[2]Craig Dykstra, *Vision and Character* (New York: Paulist Press, 1981), pp. 90-94.
[3]*Ibid*, pp. 95-98.

Relational Factors in Youth Ministry

Relational factors are not just ice-breakers. The temptation is to believe that the latter accomplish the former. Neither is a "relational model" just a programmatic model. Emphasizing relational factors as the final step of the workshop allows time to establish trust and rapport among the group. If we expect more than superficial sharing to occur, the deep interpersonal dynamics will more likely happen at the end of the process.

If the design is used with a group of adult sponsors and youth leaders, the most crucial question is how much they can trust one another and be present to one another with compassion. Craig Dykstra points out that the criterion for Christian service is not effectiveness, but *presence*.[4] The question we want to leave with participants is not "What may I do for or to these young people?" but "How may I be present with these young people in an authentic, vulnerable, compassionate, and committed way?"

While leaders must hold themselves trustworthy, that does not guarantee that they will be perceived as such by all young people. The implications point to:

1. The necessity for leaders to find affirmations in their integrity rather than in the feedback they get.
2. The importance of having more than one adult interacting with young people so that each young person may choose who will be a particular trustworthy person.

[4]*Ibid*, pp. 98-105.

Part II

Development

Chapter 3

How to Get Started

Preparation for participation in the workshop begins when people are invited to be there and take part. Preparation continues in the days before the workshop starts. The first minutes of the workshop itself take the form of orientation.

Before the Workshop

In the days before the workshop starts, information is sent about travel, housing arrangements, and the like. Materials for preparatory study are included. But it is the expectations of the participants that are most important. Here is part of a letter that was sent ahead of time to the participants in the experimental workshop:

> We hope to draw upon the reflections and interpretations of *your* experience in youth ministry as our primary resource. To begin this process of personal reflection during the next few weeks, ask yourself these questions:
>
> 1. What were two formative experiences of my youth?
> 2. What were the key influences (persons, books) during my youth?
> 3. What role did my parents play in my religious nurture? What role did the church play?
> 4. How would young people with whom you work *today* respond to the above questions?
> 5. What are two meaningful, life-giving experiences you have had in your ministry with youth? How have they shaped your present concept of ministry?
> 6. What particularities of your community are significant in working with youth?
> 7. How do you sense or determine those needs which are most pressing in the lives of your young people?
> 8. What "language" or means of expression do you use to communicate with young people.
>
> We will address these and similar questions during the days of our workshop. *You* have been chosen as a participant because of your ability to reflect and respond in creative ways. Each of you has a different role in the church's ministry, and therefore each of you represents a unique perspective. A generalization about youth in a large parish situation may not hold for youth in smaller parishes. Leadership recruitment and training may vary considerably depending on the context, yet perhaps we can discover common objectives and criteria. We will search for those elements that we share in common by recognizing the diversity of settings for ministry with youth.
>
> Come prepared to share what you have learned about yourself in laughing, crying, struggling, and growing with young people and their families. We can never expect "them" (whoever "they" are) to be more honest, self-revealing, vulnerable, spiritually attuned, or Christ-centered than we ourselves are prepared to be.
>
> By the end of the workshop we will have accomplished our goal if we have developed the following:
>
> 1. Community (having worked together as a group, aiding rather than impeding the group process)
> 2. Self-renewal for all of us in our ministry
> 3. Heightened awareness of the dynamics involved
> 4. An experiential model of learning that will be applicable for youth and adults from diverse backgrounds and settings.
> 5. A process that can be replicated
> 6. A model that engenders reflection from those

who enter the process, reflection on the goals for youth and adults engaged in ministry

Planning the First Session

The first session is for setting the tone of the workshop, getting acquainted, beginning to build a working spirit, clarifying the purposes and plan of the workshop, and introducing the elements of worship, Bible study, and personal expression, and the emphases of youth ministry and the Christian life, faith values in youth ministry, and relational factors in youth ministry. Not all of these will be stressed, but they will be there.

As we gather, O God, be in our midst as creator and sustainer, as our living redeemer, and as guiding and correcting spirit. Make us resourceful and faithful, and may our work be significant for thee.
In Jesus' name. Amen.

A simple "get acquainted" method may be used, especially if there is limited time. Just invite a response to these questions:

Who are you?
Where are you from?
What do you do?

In most cases, however, it will be much more valuable to spend a significant period of time exploring one another's backgrounds, experiences, and ideas. The following activities are designed to facilitate the process:

1. After the convener does a self-introduction, a simple procedure may be used for the participants to introduce themselves, such as the following:
   a. *Paired conversations*. Each person converses with one other person seated next to him or her. In the two or three minutes allotted (announce this ahead of time) each paired conversation should be about one or two topics. For example, "Tell each other your name, any preferred nickname you have, and the names you were called when you were a teenager. Then tell each other why you think names are important." After three minutes, ask each participant to introduce his or her partner and to tell the group one thing learned about the partner relative to names.
   b. *Four-cornered name tags*. Each person is given a piece of colored construction paper about six inches square, a dark colored crayon or marker, and a straight pin. Ask each one to make a name tag with his or her name written in large letters in the middle and with one- or two-word state-

ments written on each corner. The statements can be responses to questions such as, "What is your favorite song? Who was an adult you admired when you were young? What one or two words reflect your attitude about young people? What do you enjoy doing with young people?" It is very helpful to have these questions and a large sample of a name tag written on a large sheet of newsprint posted on the wall. After the name tags are written and pinned on each person, ask everyone to walk around the room to look at and enjoy each other's name tags.
   c. *Two truths and a fib*. The participants are given a pencil and a 4-by-6-in. card on which they are to write three statements about themselves. However, one of these statements is to be untrue. The cards are displayed on a wall or large table, and the group goes around trying to match up the cards with the right person to guess which statement is really a fib.
2. After the introductions the convener explains the general purposes of the workshop. These may be summarized with notes on a chalkboard or sheet of newsprint posted on a wall, for example:

"The workshop deals with the specific areas of youth ministry and the Christian life, faith values in youth ministry, and relational factors in youth ministry. Throughout, the elements of worship, Bible study, and personal expression will be used. The workshop can clarify the roles, relationships, and teamwork that characterize youth ministry as a pilgrimage in faith development and mutual ministry shared by youth and adults."

3. Ask the participants to share their expectations, in response to a lead-in statement such as:
    a. "This workshop will be worthwhile for me if. . . ."
    b. "A question or problem this workshop can help me resolve is. . . ."
    c. "I hope that by the time this workshop is finished. . . ."
4. Some of the statements of expectations may be noted in brief fashion on newsprint and serve throughout the workshop as a posted reminder of concerns and expectations.
5. Give an overview of the schedule, the topics that are planned for discussion, and how these may touch on the expectations of the group. Questions about the schedule, arrangements, facilities, free time, and so forth, may be answered.
6. Elicit comments on how the group expects each person to participate. Encourage each person to be responsible for his or her own learning and for attending to personal needs, but always in the light of the needs of the group. Strive in this time of orientation for "ownership" of goals and of a group-oriented style of participation. Help each person to work on becoming a member of a youth ministry team.

Introductory Bible Study

Center the introductory Bible study on Galatians 3:23–4:7. Suggest a three-step process: (1) Read the passage. (2) Ponder the passage. (3) Share questions and insights. Explain that this will be unhurried and that there may be periods when we are gathered in silence, to be broken by voiced questions or insights.

Explain that the themes of the epistle to the Galatians are justification by faith, freedom in Christ, and the universality of the gospel's appeal and claim. In the midst of the epistle, with these themes developing, comes this passage, Galatians 3:23–4:7.

Proceed to use the three-step process:

1. Read the passage (aloud and silently).
2. Ponder the passage in the gathered group in silence.
3. Share questions and insights prompted by the passage.

"Those who have ears to hear—let them hear.
This is the Word of God."

Chapter 4

Youth Ministry and the Christian Life

Personal and Communal Christian Life for God's People

The Christian life, "a Christian life-style," is a matter of concern for young persons who are in the process of deciding and acting upon their values. They are vitally interested in speaking, acting, and relating in ways which are consistent with their beliefs. Youth ministry provides young persons with opportunities to think about and to experience the Christian life in personal and communal ways.

Perhaps the most direct, clear way to describe the Christian life is to see what is said in the New Testament.

Salt, Light, Trust

"Blessed are the poor in spirit, for theirs is the kingdom of heaven. Blessed are those who mourn, for they shall be comforted. Blessed are the meek, for they shall inherit the earth. Blessed are those who hunger and thirst for righteousness, for they shall be satisfied. Blessed are the merciful, for they shall obtain mercy. Blessed are the pure in heart, for they shall see God. Blessed are the peacemakers, for they shall be called sons of God. Blessed are those who are persecuted for righteousness' sake, for theirs is the kingdom of heaven. Blessed are you when men revile you and persecute you and utter all kinds of evil against you falsely on my account. Rejoice and be glad, for your reward is great in heaven, for so men persecuted the prophets who were before you. You are the salt of the earth; but if salt has lost its taste, how shall its saltness be restored? It is no longer good for anything except to be thrown out and trodden under foot by men. You are the light of the world. A city set on a hill cannot be hid. Nor do men light a lamp and put it under a bushel, but on a stand, and it gives light to all in the house. Let your light so shine before men, that they may see your good works and give glory to your Father who is in heaven" (Matthew 5:3-16).

Among the characteristics of the Christian life are humility, compassion, meekness, concern for justice, purity, peacemaking, and speaking out for righteousness. Christians are to be the "salt of the earth" and "the light of the world." They do good works in order to glorify God.

"Therefore I tell you, do not be anxious about your life, what you shall eat or what you shall drink, nor about your body, what you shall put on. Is not life more than food, and the body more than clothing? Look at the birds of the air: they neither sow nor reap nor gather into barns, and yet your heavenly Father feeds them. Are you not of more value than they? And which of you by being anxious can add one cubit to his span of life? And why are you anxious about clothing? Consider the lilies of the field, how they grow; they neither toil nor spin; yet I tell you, even Solomon in all his glory was not

> arrayed like one of these. But if God so clothes the grass of the field, which today is alive and tomorrow is thrown into the oven, will he not much more clothe you, O men of little faith? Therefore do not be anxious, saying, 'What shall we eat?' or 'What shall we drink?' or 'What shall we wear?' For the Gentiles seek all these things; and your heavenly Father knows that you need them all. But seek first his kingdom and his righteousness, and all these things shall be yours as well. Therefore do not be anxious about tomorrow, for tomorrow will be anxious for itself. Let the day's own trouble be sufficient for the day'' (Matthew 6:25-34).

This passage states eloquently that Christians live simple lives, trusting in God's care. Christians are free from anxiety.

Grateful Response to God's Gift of Love

> Put on then, as God's chosen ones, holy and beloved, compassion, kindness, lowliness, meekness, and patience, forbearing one another and, if one has a complaint against another, forgiving each other; as the Lord has forgiven you, so you also must forgive. And above all these put on love, which binds everything together in perfect harmony. And let the peace of Christ rule in your hearts, to which indeed you were called in the one body. And be thankful. Let the word of Christ dwell in you richly, teach and admonish one another in all wisdom, and sing psalms and hymns and spiritual songs with thankfulness in your hearts to God. And whatever you do, in word or deed, do everything in the name of the Lord Jesus, giving thanks to God the Father through him (Colossians 3:12-17).

The Christian life is expressed as a grateful response to God's gift of love. This is an important distinction of the Christian motivation for why and how life is lived. What we do is not in order to gain something for ourselves, but as a *response* to what God has done already and continues to do for us. We act out of a sense of gratitude. The passage from Colossians describes such a life as one in which ''the peace of Christ rules in your heart,'' and in which every action is done ''in the name of Christ.''

An Ethical Life

> From now on, therefore, we regard no one from a human point of view; even though we once regarded Christ from a human point of view, we regard him thus no longer. Therefore, if any one is in Christ, he is a new creation; the old has passed away, behold, the new has come. All this is from God, who through Christ reconciled us to himself and gave us the ministry of reconciliation; that is, in Christ God was reconciling the world to himself, not counting their trespasses against them, and entrusting to us the message of reconciliation. So we are ambassadors for Christ, God making his appeal through us. We beseech you on behalf of Christ, be reconciled to God. For our sake he made him to be sin who knew no sin, so that in him we might become the righteousness of God (2 Corinthians 5:16-21).

The Christian life is ethical. As ''new creations'' seeking to live in a ''new order,'' we try to be ''ambassadors for Christ'' and ''agents of Christ's reconciliation.'' This passage in 2 Corinthians touches on a theme that receives great emphasis in the New Testament, that of ministry. Christians serve other people through their prayers, witness, deeds of service, and activities on behalf of justice.

Discipleship

> When they had finished breakfast, Jesus said to Simon Peter, ''Simon, son of John, do you love me more than these?'' He said to him, ''Yes, Lord; you know that I love you.'' He said to him, ''Feed my lambs.'' A second time he said to him, ''Simon, son of John, do you love me?'' He said to him, ''Yes, Lord; you know that I love you.'' He said to him, ''Tend my sheep.'' He said to him the third time,''Simon, son of John, do you love me?'' Peter was grieved because he said to him the third time, ''Do you love me?'' And he said to him, ''Lord, you know everything; you know that I love you.'' Jesus said to him, ''Feed my sheep'' (John 21:15-17).

The Christian life is one of discipleship. We believe that Jesus Christ calls us to be his followers. Further, we believe that because Jesus Christ loves us, our appropriate response is to share this love with others.

Youth's Calling

Young persons, as a part of the church, are called to discipleship and to the Christian life. The goals of youth ministry reflect this calling. The program provides practical ways to fulfill it. In a more critical tone it may be said that youth ministry is more than fun and games to entertain young persons and to keep them in the church. Youth ministry is *ministry*—servanthood, service, sacrifice, and even suffering. It is the task of leaders who work with youth to communicate the call to discipleship. In many quarters this task has been neglected, and young persons have not been informed of this risky and difficult aspect of the Christian life. However, there is a renewal of the conviction that where the challenge has been presented forthrightly, young persons have responded with commitment. Where the challenge has not been present, young persons in those situations often have found the church wanting in conviction and purpose and have left the church to seek growth and challenge elsewhere.

An integral understanding of the Christian life is that it is both personal and communal. Personal piety is balanced with corporate relationships and mutual responsibility. Each individual Christian joins with others to act corporately, striving to be the example of a wholesome community, and to be a strong force in addressing the social concerns of life in the world.

Workshop Activities

For adult leaders (including pastors, leaders of youth groups, teachers, and parents): The activities suggested here are designed to help adult leaders of youth reflect on their own Christian lives in the church and in the world, and to prepare them to help young persons lead Christian lives. The activities call attention to role models and values the leaders encountered during their own adolescence, and how these contributed to an understanding of the Christian life.

For youth: These same activities can help youth reflect in similar ways and prepare them for more effective leadership in ministry with other youth.

The activities include handouts that are to be used by each participant. Duplicate enough copies so that each participant has one.

(Note: The activities on youth ministry and the Christian life are based on a design by Freda Gardner, Associate Professor of Christian Education, Princeton Theological Seminary.)

Adolescent Heroes and Villains

Distribute the handout "Adolescent Heroes and Villains."

Ask each person to think about the categories listed in the handout, and then to fill in the blanks.

Either as an entire group or in small groups of three persons, have the participants share some of the things they have written. Ask: "What do your responses suggest about how persons find out what is meant by the Christian life?" Suggest that they give examples.

Ask: "Whom did your family or community identify as heroes or villains? Can you trace any of your adolescent behavior patterns to these examples?"

You as an Adolescent

Distribute the handout "You as an Adolescent."

Ask each person to fill in the blanks.

Form groups of three. Discuss the answers.

Ask: "What do your answers suggest about how personal, family, and community expectations influenced our behavior patterns as adolescents?"

Ask: "What does this indicate about how adolescents develop personal values?"

Keeping or Dropping Values

Distribute the handout "Keeping or Dropping Values."

Ask the participants to fill in the blanks. Note that one set of questions is for adults and another set for young persons of junior or senior high school age.

In groups of three, discuss the results. The difficult question here is why certain values that are deemed important during adolescence are kept, while others are dropped. Keeping a value implies that a person is patterning behavior according to that value. Dropping a value means a corresponding change in behavior.

Ask: "What roles do various institutions play in helping a person to maintain certain values and pattern behavior according to them—the family, friends, the church, for instance?"

Ask: "How, in an ideal youth ministry setting, may the church help young persons to define Christian values and the Christian life? How may the church foster the practice of the Christian life?"

Biblical Descriptions of the Christian Life

Hand out copies of "Personal and Communal Christian Life for God's People." (From pages 29-31 in this manual.)

Either stay together as a group for the following activity, *or* divide into five small groups, each to concentrate on one of the Bible passages.

Ask: "What aspects of the Christian life are described in each passage?"

"What aspects of the Christian life are personal in nature?"

"What aspects of the Christian life are corporate in nature, or call for corporate expression?"

"How may the Christian life be described in

ways that are appropriate for young persons?''
''How may our youth ministry foster these aspects of the Christian life?''

Comparing Components of the Christian Life

Distribute the handout ''Comparing Components of the Christian Life.''

Ask the participants to jot down their notes on the handout.

Engage in a general discussion of the questions on the handout, using newsprint to record the ideas that come from the discussion.

Ask: ''In light of the tensions that have been brought out, is it possible to establish a general description of the Christian life, or must there be allowance to a range of expression of what the Christian life is?''

Concluding Question

Ask: ''What insights have we gained on how to deal with the Christian life in youth ministry?''

Record these insights on newsprint (perhaps asking each person to record his or her own). Leave the newsprint up for the group to come back to later in the session.

Worship

Include in your worship the following prayer:

O God, who dost open the Christian life to us, and who dost call us to it, enable us to weigh values carefully, and to be guided by those values that contribute most to personal and corporate faithfulness. Open us also to new insights on how our youth ministry may become an instrument of faithfulness for us and for those whom we seek to lead.

In Jesus' name. Amen.

Use the hymn ''O Master, Let Me Walk with Thee.''

Handout: ADOLESCENT HEROES AND VILLAINS

Real or fictional heroes or villains of your adolescence	Characteristics and qualities that captured your attention	Your responses: relational, modeling, imagining, etc.

Handout: YOU AS AN ADOLESCENT

For youth:

How do you see yourself? What do you think of yourself?

What are your most important values, ideals, or goals?

How do these values manifest themselves or show up in your life?

What barriers prevent their manifestation? To what extent may these barriers be real or imagined?

For adults:

How did you see yourself? What did you think of yourself?

What were your most important values, ideals, or goals?

How did these values manifest themselves or show up in your life?

What barriers prevented their manifestation? Did these barriers turn out to be real or imagined?

Handout: KEEPING OR DROPPING VALUES

For adults:

Which of your adolescent values have been carried into adulthood?

For what reasons have some adolescent values been dropped?

For what reasons have some adolescent values been retained but not yet incorporated into your adult life?

For youth:

Which of your present values do you expect to continue into your adult life?

Which values do you expect will be dropped in the next 10-20 years?

What do you anticipate as difficulties in living with your values as an adult?

Handout: COMPARING COMPONENTS OF THE CHRISTIAN LIFE

A. What biblical stories or images describe characteristics of a Christian life-style?

B. What aspects of one's life might be considered as the components of life-style?

D. Identify tension points in a Christian community that might include such diversities of expressions as named in C.

C. In at least one aspect/component from B, identify some of the range of expressions of a Christian life-style that would incorporate the characteristics listed in A.

Chapter 5

Faith Values in Youth Ministry

Faith Pilgrimage

A young person's experience of identity formation may also be an experience of value formation and faith development. Adolescence may be a journey or a quest, or in religious terms, a faith pilgrimage. During childhood, information about traditions, beliefs, and religious practices is learned. During young adulthood, people act upon decisions about careers, life partners, and community responsibilities. In between childhood and adulthood, adolescents engage in a search for values, beliefs, and commitments that they may call their own. This search may be relatively uncomplicated for some; for many it is a long journey with a puzzling mixture of joyful discoveries, sad disappointments, times of loneliness, and moments of blessed community. It is a time of experimentation and learning by trial and error.

Journey in Faith

A faith pilgrimage takes the seeker beyond knowledge about matters of faith—knowledge about God, about the church, about the Bible—into the realm of faithfulness. Somehow the pilgrim, who goes about seeking values and faith, becomes one blessed with faith. Faith is a gift given by God! Those who seek faith discover that faith becomes theirs as a gift. Adolescents, who are capable now of abstract thinking, are able to discover that faith is not a ''thing'' or a set of doctrines to learn, but that faith is a relationship. They are able to say that God loves them and relates with them. To trust and enjoy this loving relationship is to have faith.

The church's opportunity for ministry is found in the realization that the teenage years are very appropriate times for persons to be on a faith pilgrimage. While they are working on the tasks of identity, value formation, and establishing independence, young persons ought to be encouraged to ask questions, to doubt previously given answers, and ultimately to arrive at their own conclusions about life, values, and faith.

Pilgrimage with Youth

To have adults walking along with young persons on a faith pilgrimage is a very good form of ministry. Adults have much they can offer to the young pilgrim. The adults may also discover, happily, that the young pilgrims have ways of seeing and explaining that give new visions to the older pilgrims! In youth ministry adults can walk with young persons, sometimes leading, sometimes pushing, and sometimes being led and being ministered unto. Youth ministry can be a shared pilgrimage.

Convictions That Shape Choices and Affect Actions

Faith values are convictions or beliefs that shape our choices and affect our actions. Consider these three assumptions:

- As people of God our values are molded by biblical stories and biblical insights.
- Unless leaders are willing to deal with personal experiences (personal stories), they cannot minister with youth.

- As Christians we have a central story: the Christ event.

Stories are useful in a relation-centered youth ministry program. To tell our stories and to try to interpret these in the light of the Christian story is a forceful way to come to grips with our own faith values.

Workshop Activities

The workshop activities reflect the three assumptions that have just been noted.

Designed both for adult leaders (including pastors, leaders of youth groups, teachers, and parents) and for youth, the activities form a sequence in which we explore our stories in the light of the Christian story, seeking guidance on ways in which we may help others to do the same thing.

(Note: The activities on faith values in youth ministry are based on a design created by Stephen F. Boehlke, Director, Alive, a ministry of nurture and healing care responding especially to the needs of young adults, Ridgewood, New Jersey.)

Telling a Story Around the Circle

A way to begin a workshop section on faith values, through the device of telling our stories and being confronted by the stories of the Bible, is to tell a story around the circle. This provides a simple example and gets everyone involved quickly. Provide a situation, such as a common interpersonal dilemma, and ask the group to complete the story, with each person in the circle adding a paragraph to it. Once the story has "gone around the circle," ask the group to think about an appropriate ending. Share various versions of how the story might end.

Here is a dilemma to start the story:

> Forrest really likes Camellia very much, but before he can get up the courage to ask her to the junior prom, Lily invites Forrest to the prom. Forrest's father advises him to accept Lily's invitation, but Forrest's mother and his younger sister, Pansy, tell him that is old-fashioned and that he should assert himself and do whatever he wishes. At this point Forrest calls his best friend, Woody, who says. . . .

Inventing the story around the circle should be done with a light touch—make it an enjoyable activity! At the conclusion, however, ask the group to select from the story several points of analysis:

1. What are some of the social customs and social values that were operative behind the story?
2. For all the intricacies (and perhaps zaniness) of this story-in-the-round, what is the basic problem? (There will be different opinions about the answer to this question.)
3. Who hindered and who helped in attempting to resolve the problem?

As a surprise the leader may want to inject this question: "Where is God in this story?"

The question "Where is God in this story?" pushes the group to consider a way of interpreting stories. As Christians we believe that God is present in our lives. Through the situations and dilemmas we experience, we discover that we have learned, have grown, have become more (or less) faithful. Often, in hindsight, we can say in faith that God has been at work in our lives. Looking back on our life events, we discern how we have been guided by certain values and doctrines, and how certain persons and institutions have influenced us. Those who are members of the faith community then go on to say that in all these things God has been present in our lives.

A discussion of the question "Where is God in this story?" may lead to a consensus about a principle of interpretation: *Our stories reveal our values.*

In the Christian tradition, stories have taken on great importance, for it is through stories that we have tried to communicate our beliefs—the Bible is our story of who God is and what God has done to create, sustain, and redeem a people and a creation. We can discern God's activity in the stories found in the Bible, and we can discern God's activity in our own stories. Comparing our stories with those of the Bible further helps us to discern the demanding and merciful love of God.

Reflecting on Bible Stories and Personal Stories

This activity revolves around three questions that the participants answer by jotting notes on sheets of paper and then discussing their responses in the group. The questions are:

- What Bible story affirms for you some good news about youth ministry?
- What story from your own experience of youth ministry conveys some good news?
- What words or phrases express the faith values found in each story?

Ask the first question and have the group work on it,

then ask the second question, and so forth, to avoid trying to do too much at one time.

Provide an example of a Bible story because there will be those who are not familiar with the Bible or who have never dealt with biblical material in this way. For example, tell the story of David and Goliath and interpret it as an account of a young person who was called from one field of endeavor—tending sheep—to another, being a liberator. Or tell the story of Jesus' appearance with the disciples on the beach after the resurrection. Tell how Jesus confronted Peter with the same command three times: Feed my sheep. Interpret this as a symbolic form of forgiving Peter for having denied Jesus three times, and as a form of commissioning Peter to ministry in Christ's name. This is good news about youth ministry for those who feel they have failed Jesus and are not worthy of being disciples.

To facilitate the participants' work on biblical and personal stories, provide plenty of paper and pencils, and also some Bibles. With each question allow time for each person to think about an answer and to jot notes on paper. During the group discussion, jot on a posted sheet of newsprint the responses that have been shared. In discussing the third question, jot down the word or phrases which are offered, like this:

Don—"becoming teachable"
Wayne—"laughter"
Dave—"friends"
Jean—"I believe, help my unbelief"
Marlene—"community support during crisis"
Bob—"recalcitrant prophet"
Roger—"wrestling with God"

In the concluding discussion, attempt to consider how the participants' selection of stories, biblical and personal, imply their goals for youth ministry. For example, using our own armor, our own gifts, rather than what others put on us, as Saul attempted to put *his* armor on young David.

Ask the participants to consider how they can identify "the Christ event" or the presence of God in some of the stories that were told. (What is intended here is the use of a principle of interpretation in which Christians interpret events and the stories of the Bible, through faith. Christian values and beliefs are avoided or not understood by many in the churches because this principle of interpretation is not used.)

How the World Challenges Our Faith Values

Having told biblical stories and personal stories from the perspective of how these stories affirm our faith values, it is well to look further at the stories in terms of how the world, especially the world of youth, challenges these faith values. This is not to set up a simple "us *vs.* them" situation, implying that Christians are "good guys" and that the world consists of "bad guys," but to realize that Christian values and beliefs are not universally understood or accepted, and that Christians need to be clear about their beliefs and values and able to articulate them. Our faith values do not deserve our acceptance unless they can stand up to rigorous criticism and be stated with coherence and integrity.

Ask members of the group to review in their own minds the stories and the words and phrases which have been shared in the previous activity. Ask them to imagine this material being shared in a typical setting "in the world," that is in life outside the bounds of the institutional church. How would people who do not share our commitments respond to these stories and words? What questions and challenges would they express?

Hand out 3-by-5-in. cards and pencils and ask each person to write a question or challenge on a card. If someone has more than one challenge, write them all down, one challenge per card. The challenges might look like this:

- David and Goliath lived in simple times—teenagers today live in a world with no simple answers.

- Christians tend to be "cockeyed optimists."

- If God really has been active in their lives, young people have no way of knowing it.

- Most jobs today could hardly be considered "a Christian calling."

Collect the cards with challenges written on them, and hand them out again so that each person gets a challenge card written by someone else. Each person then reads aloud the challenge and tries to respond to it. After each person has had a turn, the group discusses the challenges and responses which are of particular interest to persons in the group.

In concluding this portion of the discussion, ask: "What opinions do you have about what makes it difficult for young persons to understand Christian faith values? Why do you think it is hard for young persons to live by them? What type of youth ministry program might help young persons develop their faith values?"

"Test Yourselves"

Divide into groups of three or four and read 2 Corinthians, chapters 5-10. Ask: "What does Paul mean by asking 'Do you not realize that God is in you?' In what ways is it appropriate for us, personally and together, to 'examine ourselves, to see whether we are holding to our faith?' How do we know whether we have passed the test, or failed? In what ways is improvement called for? What do you suppose led Paul to say what he did in verse 10?"

Still in groups of three or four, read Hebrews 4:12. How does this add to, or change, your concept of "the Word of God"? How does such an interpretation point to the relation of the Word of God to our faith values? How do you suggest that our faith values be tested by the Word of God?

Faith Values Central to Youth Ministry

A way to draw some conclusions about the entire discussion of stories, faith, beliefs, and values, is to have the groups work on two questions:

What beliefs and faith values can be added to our list of values discussed so far?
What faith values are central to my understanding of youth ministry?

In reviewing the words and phrases that express our faith values, listed in an earlier activity, the group may come up with additional items that round out the list so that it is more comprehensive and balanced, covering the major aspects of the Christian faith. Words such as community, acceptance, forgiveness, sacrifice, service, stewardship, pilgrimage of faith, and humility may be listed.

Ask each person in considering the second question to see this as an opportunity to begin to state the rationale or goals for youth ministry. For example, someone might come up with a list such as this:

Acceptance of God's grace
Pilgrimage of faith
Caring-covenanting community
Discipleship, servanthood

Ask the participants to ponder what these concise lists imply about youth ministry in the congregation. Or ask them to ponder what *vision* of youth ministry emerges from these lists.

Concluding Questions

Ask: "What about adding our story as a church to the 'personal story-Bible story' encounter? Our story as a family?"
"How may faith values be expressed in language and other ways which are more appropriate to youth?"

Record your ideas on these questions on newsprint, and leave the newsprint up to review from time to time.

Worship

Include in your worship the following prayer:

Teach us, O God, the ways of faith and faithfulness. Lead us to the sources of faith, and help us to know the truth that sets both us and our neighbors free. Deepen and sharpen, throughout our whole faith pilgrimage, the values we hold and by which we seek to live. And with added clarity and power, make us useful to others as they look for the road of faith, as they find it, and as they journey in it.

In Jesus' name. Amen.

Use the hymn "Spirit of God, Descend upon My Heart."

Chapter 6

Relational Factors in Youth Ministry

The Ministry of Relationships

Workshop Activities

Some Things About Myself
Chart of Religious and Personal Life
Significant Persons During My Adolescence
What Would You Do?
Axioms of Trust Relationships
Concluding Questions

Handouts

The Ministry of Relationships

The theme of relationships has pervaded the explorations of the Christian life and of faith values, since the crux of youth ministry is the way we relate to God, to ourselves, and to each other as peers and across the generations. Ministry consists of a complex of relationships.

Relationships and Self-Identity

A common understanding of what is happening in the lives of young persons of junior and senior high school age is that they are involved in the task of identity formation. They are working on forming a sense of who they are in the light of their personal and family backgrounds, their perceptions of how others view them, and their personal definitions of themselves. This very personal task is approached uniquely by each individual and yet is also a very social task. Peers and significant adults greatly influence a person forming an identity. During the adolescent years people need others for support, listening, guidance, and even for occasional comic relief—for the touch of humor that helps them to see themselves in comparison with others who are equally at sea.

Relating Personally

Adults and older youth working with young persons can be of profound help in personal ways: sharing, friendship, caring, listening, offering suggestions and guidance, and offering themselves as examples or models of personal formation of identity and of Christian life. They can be guarantors.

One of the greatest gifts a leader can offer is a trust relationship. Beyond the structure and programs that comprise youth ministry there are relationships of this kind. As young persons and adults move beyond acquaintanceship to trusting relationships, the opportunities arise for caring and for sharing faith.

The Leader's Own Relationships and Self-Identity

In order to relate well with others, leaders need an awareness of their own selves. They must themselves reflect on personal development and identity formation. Leaders need to recognize persons who were influential in their identity formation, how they were influential, and how they, themselves, might in turn seek to influence young persons today. In order to relate with young persons, leaders need to appreciate the relationships that nurtured, supported, and provided models for their own growth.

Workshop Activities

The workshop activities are designed as means for exploration of how we came to be who we are through relationships with others (other individuals, family members, the church, the community, and God), who we now conceive ourselves to have come to be, how our relationships are developing and growing, and how we may (through relationships) be effective in youth ministry.

The activities are designed for adult leaders (including pastors, leaders of youth groups, teachers, and parents) and for youth to use together or separately. The design is such that through the use of these activities, relationships may not only be explored and identified, but also developed and enhanced.

(Note: The activities on relational factors in youth ministry are based on a design by Roger Uittenbogaard, Trinity United Presbyterian Church, Cherry Hill, New Jersey.)

Some Things About Myself

Distribute the handout "Some Things About Myself."

Ask each participant to fill in boxes 1,2, and 3 first, and then go back and fill in box 4 (corresponding to 1), box 5 (corresponding to 2), and box 6 (corresponding to 3). Explain that these things will be shared and discussed.

Either in the full group, or in smaller groups of three or four, share what has been written in boxes 1 and 4. Using newsprint to record them and to sort them out, decide on what seem to be the kinds of relationships that help us to identify ourselves.

Continuing in the same grouping, share what has been written in boxes 2 and 5. Use newsprint to record the results and to sort them out. Ask: "What are the kinds of relationships that seem to make life events significant?"

In the same grouping again, share what you have written in boxes 3 and 6. Record the results and sort them out, using newsprint. Ask: "What are the kinds of relationships that seem to be important in youth ministry?"

If you have been working in small groups, come back into the full group again. Ask: "What qualities seem to make certain relationships more significant and influential than others?"

Chart of Religious and Personal Life

Distribute the handout "Religious and Personal Life Graph." Explain how each person may sketch on it a graph of his or her religious and personal life development. (Assure the participants that they will not be asked to show the results to anyone else, but that there will be an opportunity after personal reflection to tell others whatever they wish to tell and, of course, not to tell whatever they choose to keep to themselves.)

The numbered horizontal line represents a time line of one's life history from birth to the present time. The plus (+) and minus (−) signs represent highlights or low points in one's life.

Have each person use a continuous line (________) to draw on the chart an approximation of his or her personal life, showing the degree to which life was on the "plus" side or on the "minus" side at each stage. If, for instance, life was very difficult and on the negative side, the drawn line would be toward the double minus (− −) section of the scale. If, on the other hand, life were extremely rewarding and fruitful at a given point, the drawn line would be toward the double plus (+ +) section of the scale. To draw this personal life line, one needs to recall key events and relationships in each decade of life.

In similar fashion, have each person use a dotted line (_ _ _ _ _) to chart an approximation of his or her religious development.

Once the charts are completed, ask each person to reflect on what has been sketched:

- Does a pattern of development emerge?
- Are certain types of events prominent in one's life?
- What might be said about the positive events?
- About the negative events?
- Is there any correlation between personal and religious life?
- Focusing on the years between ten and twenty, what observations may be made?
- How do these years look in the context of one's whole life?

In this portion of the activity, allow time for personal reflection. If some persons begin to talk about their own charts, let the conversation develop spontaneously.

Reassuring the participants that they are free to say as little or as much as they wish, run through the questions again, inviting them to share observations and learnings.

Conclude by inviting them to venture some hunches or generalizations about personal and religious development and about the influences during adolescence that seem to be significant.

Significant Persons During My Adolescence

A way to dig deeply into the matter of how significant adults may influence young persons is to concentrate on writing lists of the characteristics of those who were significant to the participants when they were adolescents. A list might look like this:

Like a father figure
Related as an adult friend (guarantor, role model)
Committed Christian

Creative
Not afraid to reach out and touch
Had sense of humor—could laugh at self
Willing to take risks

Ask the participants to think about their adolescent years, and to list at least three persons who were influential in their development. Under each name list that person's influential characteristics, or list *how* that person was influential. In the general discussion ask the participants to try to identify the areas of life that are receptive to the influence of another person, how influence is conveyed, and how each person might want to be influential among young persons today.

A discussion of the characteristics that emerge from the various lists may identify characteristics in adults that young persons seek, and issues in the lives of adolescents concerning which they seek support or guidance.

What Would You Do?

This activity considers ways in which trusting relationships may be built between young persons and adults.

Give each person a copy of the handout "What Would You Do?"

Ask each to write brief answers.

Pair off. Have each pair choose the situations in which they are most interested and role-play them.

In the general discussion following each role play, ask the group members to share ways they would propose to deal with the situations, and then to indicate how responses to these typical situations lead toward or away from relationships of trust.

As a concluding question, ask: "What characterizes a trusting relationship between a young person and an adult?"

Axioms of Trust Relationships

Distribute the handout "Axioms of Trust Relationships."

Allow adequate time for individual reading of the twenty-two axioms.

Ask each person to check the axioms that he or she feels would be really useful in the particular youth ministry in which he or she is presently engaged.

Then ask them to review the axioms that they have checked, and to *double-check* the *five* axioms they consider to be most indispensable.

Divide into groups of three, compare the lists of the five most indispensable axioms and, as a group, rank the most indispensable axioms from the most indispensable to the least. Be prepared to give examples from your experience with youth or in youth ministry.

In the total group share the results. Then ask: "What, in your individual opinion, does this add up to?"

At the end, ask: "How, then, may youth-adult relationships be an effective form of ministry? How may we actually conduct a youth ministry of relationships?"

Concluding Questions

Offer these questions to the group, leaving time between them for thoughtful silence and for several brief answers.

What about various personalities and the ways they color relationships?
What about relationship to God, Christ, the Spirit, as individuals and as groups?
What about relationships with the church?
What networks of relationships are important?
What about the relationships of leaders to one another?
How does one improve and enrich relationships?
How does one "train" for relationships?
How may the circle of relationships be enlarged to include the poor, the oppressed, and the victims of injustice?
How may the circle of relationships be enlarged to include the decision makers in society and culture?

Worship

Include the following prayer:

O God, what may we call thee—father, mother, brother, sister, friend, leader, shepherd? We reach out to others, to touch and to be touched, to know them and to be known by them, and to call them by name. Thou dost reach out to us in creating us, in redeeming us in Jesus Christ, and in leading, correcting, and supporting us by thy Holy Spirit. Enable us, with the youth in our care, to reach out to thee, to touch thee, to know thee, and to call thee by name.

In Jesus' name. Amen.

Use the hymn "Jesus, Friend of Thronging Pilgrims."

Jesus, Friend of Thronging Pilgrims

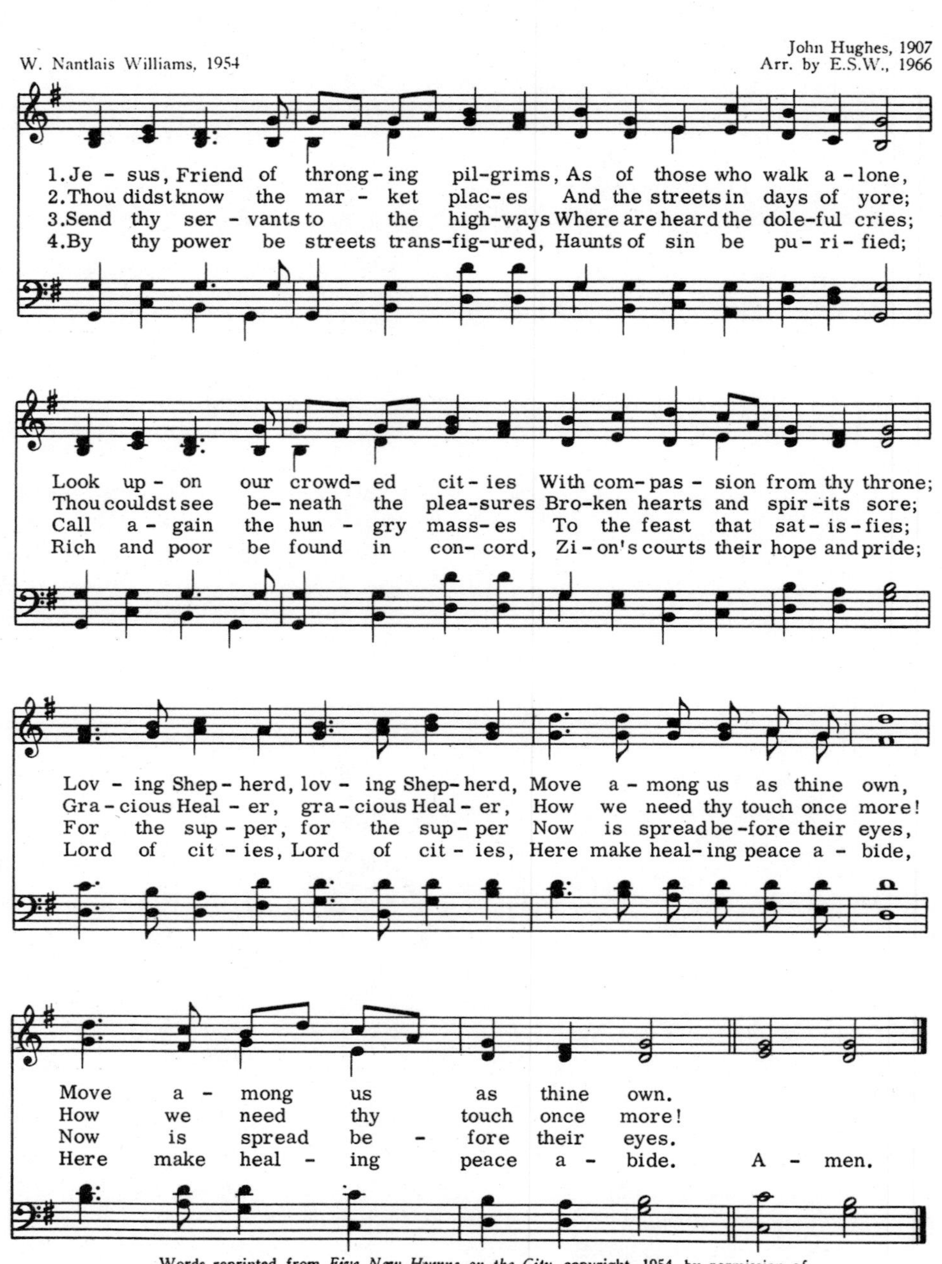

Words reprinted from *Five New Hymns on the City*, copyright, 1954, by permission of The Hymn Society of America. Tune used by permission of Dilys S. Webb.

Handout: SOME THINGS ABOUT MYSELF

1. You are with a group of people whom you know only casually. You would like to know them better. What would you say to introduce yourself to them?	4. What relationships are involved in what you have said about yourself?
2. Describe one event in your life history that stands out as being very important.	5. What persons or relationships made this event so important to you?
3. What are the main reasons you are interested in youth ministry?	6. What kinds of relationships are essential for you in youth ministry? What relationships do you hope to enhance through youth ministry?

Handout: RELIGIOUS AND PERSONAL LIFE GRAPH

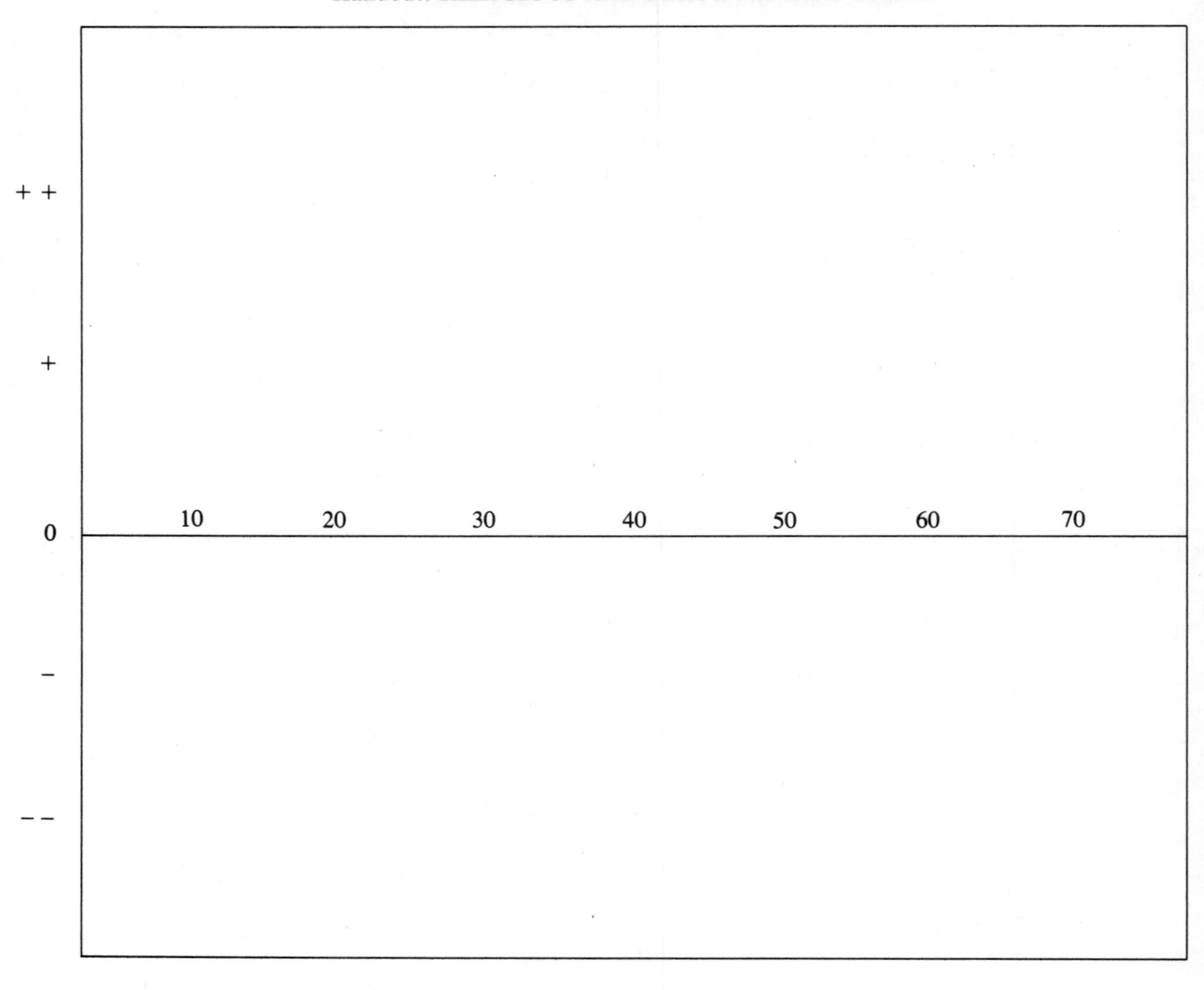

Religious life = ________________________________

Personal life = _____ _____ _____ _____ _____ _____

Handout: WHAT WOULD YOU DO?

Imagine that a member of your youth group needs help in each of the situations below. Indicate what you would do if you were asked for help or advice in each of the situations.

If someone asked me:

1. To help pick out new clothes.
2. To help with school homework.
3. To help choose courses to take.
4. To talk because he or she is feeling upset.
5. To talk about a sexual experience that has made him or her uncomfortable.
6. To talk about having been caught breaking a law.
7. To help find a part-time job.
8. To talk about his or her religious beliefs.
9. To talk about his or her feelings about the death of a friend or relative.
10. To talk about problems with a friend.
11. To help him or her decide what to do after graduating from high school.

Handout: AXIOMS OF TRUST RELATIONSHIPS

1. A first step in a trust relationship is knowing someone's name.
2. Ideally, the people in the group gradually begin to like and trust one another.
3. Before a person can benefit from counseling, a precounseling relationship can be built through group activities.
4. The group leader is obliged to be worthy of the group's trust.
5. The youth leader gradually builds a reputation among young people and adults as a trustworthy person.
6. The adult leader gives more to a trust relationship than a teenager does.
7. An intermediate stage in a trust relationship is active listening, which requires reserving judgments while helping a person to clarify his or her own needs and goals.
8. The trust relationship need not be verbalized.
9. Young persons in trust relationships help themselves; the youth leader doesn't do things for them.
10. The need for trust relationships varies from one person to another.
11. At a given time, members of the group will be in various stages of trust relationships.
12. Some aspects of people's lives should be allowed to remain private.
13. A crisis can cause a person to skip steps in the trust relationship.
14. In a crisis the youth leader may need to refer young persons to other adults.
15. Without realistic goals and the support of other adults, adult leaders are likely to burn out.
16. A youth leader's own needs can reinforce or distort trust relationships.
17. Trust relationships can bring problems to the surface that were hidden, sometimes making a youth leader appear to be a troublemaker.
18. Group influence can encourage or discourage trust relationships.
19. A group should be open to all kinds of people, yet it needs a core of persons who can be trusted to take some responsibility for the group.
20. When the number of isolated or antisocial persons in a group increases, the chances of losing group members also increase.
21. Trust relationships are not easily quantifiable; large turnouts for events may be counterproductive.
22. Trust relationships within the group nourish good relationships in the family, school, church, and community.

Part III

Culmination

Chapter 7

Pulling It Together

By the closing session of the workshop, the participants will have deepened their personal grasp of youth ministry as a dynamic process. The concept of youth ministry will be more specific and more meaningful to them, and the call to minister with youth will have been sharpened and clarified.

All of these aspects may now be pulled together—not to finish them off, but so that they may be incorporated into present and future youth ministries. The understandings and insights that persons have gained, the relationships that they have developed, the friendships that have been formed, and the convictions that participants are ready to adopt and use need to be recognized, voiced, shared, and celebrated.

Planning for the Last Session

The last session is so important that it needs to be a continuing concern of the steering committee and the designated leaders throughout the workshop. Anticipating that session, members of the steering committee serve as a "listening team," staying alert to what people are saying, doing, and feeling. They make themselves sensitive to questions, problems, concerns, relationships, insights, convictions, and intentions on the part of the participants.

The designated leaders contribute not only what they have done, but also their feelings about the responses to what they have done and to both expected and unexpected outcomes of their work as those outcomes have emerged. The leaders in the areas of worship, Bible study, personal expression, youth ministry and the Christian life, faith values in youth ministry, and relational factors in youth ministry, all have large investments in what they have done and in what has taken place and developed out of what they have done.

So the steering committee and the designated leaders have to be thinking and planning together throughout the event for the richest and most meaningful ways of bringing the workshop to a climax.

That climax will probably have four segments:

1. A session in which questions, problems, concerns, relationships, insights, convictions, and intentions are shared. (Let the designated leaders for youth ministry and the Christian life, faith values in youth ministry, and relational factors in youth ministry take responsibility for planning this segment, calling on others as they choose.)
2. A session for evaluation. (Let the steering committee take responsibility for planning this segment, calling on others as they choose.)
3. A session to consider various possibilities for the future, growing out of the workshop. (Let the steering committee take responsibility for planning this segment, calling on others as they choose.)
4. A session for celebrating the event. (Let the designated leaders for worship, Bible study, and personal expression take responsibility for planning this segment, calling on others as they choose.)

What is here envisioned is a full and rather elaborate experience, culminating a rich and meaningful event, and growing out of that event rather than being artificial and preplanned.

Alternatives

The workshop may have developed in such a way that a simpler experience would be more appropriate.

The participants will be helped if they can review activities, state the main learnings, and express their intentions to practice their learnings "back home." A way to obtain such closure is to ask the participants to recall the main topics and procedures used, then in their own minds to identify what from those discussions they found to be helpful (or which raised questions). The leader may ask, for example, "What was one thing you learned about relationships in youth ministry? How will you do youth ministry differently?"

Thomas Groome in *Christian Religious Education*[1] suggests what he calls "shared Christian praxis," a process that has been used in modified form elsewhere in the workshop plan. How it may be used in a very personal way to summarize and direct what has been learned about preparing youth and adults for youth ministry, may be put in the following five steps:

1. Naming our present action
   - Who are we as ministers with youth?
   - What youth ministry are we carrying on?
   - Where are our strengths and weaknesses, our successes and failures?
2. Sharing our stories
   - Here we talk with each other about our actual experiences in youth ministry.
   - And we talk about our experiences in the workshop.
3. Hearing the Story
   - Here we open ourselves to listen to the gospel.
   - How does the gospel speak to our experiences in youth ministry?
   - How does the gospel speak to our experiences in the workshop?
4. Sharing our visions
   - Here we talk with each other about our hopes and visions for youth ministry, and for ourselves as youth ministers.
   - And we talk about the hopes and visions that are associated for us with the workshop.
5. Hearing the Vision
   - Here we open ourselves to listen to the gospel.
   - How does the gospel speak to our hopes and visions for youth ministry?
   - How does the gospel speak to the hopes and visions that are associated for us with the workshop?

Evaluation

Some form of evaluation can take place as the workshop draws to a close. There are a number of effective ways to evaluate, including referring to the expectations listed at the beginning of the workshop, or filling out a form with questions to be answered. The form can use questions to be answered by checking a number on a scale. ("On a scale of 1 to 5, with 1 being high and 5 being low, how would you rate the discussion of youth ministry and the Christian life?")

Evaluations can be quite informal, too. The leader asks the group members what they found helpful, what could have been improved, and what they hope to use in their own youth ministries in the future. Whatever process is used for evalutation, the intention is to allow the participants to express themselves, and to guide planning of similar workshops in the future.

Closing

If the workshop is being held in a weekend retreat setting, it is likely that it will end with lunch. It may be appropriate to conclude with a Bible reading, perhaps the same passage which was read at the beginning of the workshop. This time there is no need for a group discussion of the passage, even if a few minutes are given for personal reflection and meditation and then for prayer.

A simple ritual at the end can be the final group activity—each person can offer a benediction to someone standing next to him or her. The leader starts this concluding activity by giving a traditional benediction and asking each person to offer to a few others a blessing such as this: "My hope for you as youth leader is. . . . " A handshake or similar passing of the peace accompanies the blessing.

"By the end of the workshop, a spirit of teamwork in ministry was realized. Not only did we learn about relationships, faith, and Christian life-style, we developed friendships, shared our own faith questions, and lived in Christian community."

—a member of the experimental workshop

[1] Thomas Groome, *Christian Religious Education* (San Francisco: Harper & Row, Publishers, Inc., 1980).

Chapter 8

Following It Up

Identifying a goal, three elements (worship, Bible study, and personal expression), and three emphases (youth ministry and the Christian life, faith values in youth ministry, and relational factors in youth ministry), the workshop plan provides a focus for the energies that are being expended by leaders of youth. Once through the material is probably not enough. The process is replicable, so that with a change of material and activities it may be used at more advanced levels with more and more experienced people, as well as adapted within the general framework to the needs of various groups who are just beginning youth ministry, or who may even be at the preliminary stage of considering the possibility of youth ministry.

The process does not rely on specialists or on individual expertise, although they can greatly enhance it. Basically it calls to the fore youth leaders' commitments and their willingness to learn about themselves in relation to young people.

There is a timeliness about such workshops. Churches are searching for ways to enhance (and sometimes even to rescue) their youth ministry programs. Here is a theoretical framework and a relational process to complement the numerous programmatic models coming on the scene. Our efforts have been directed at an overall approach to *ministry* with youth. It is this ministry which is the life-giving constant, as evidenced by the self-renewal experienced at our recent workshop.

The strategy for recommitment is one of rediscovery by youth and leaders of youth together of our needs for and gifts in ministry, and mutual expansion of our self-awareness in relation to these needs and gifts by getting at our biblical and spiritual rootage in Christ. This process of self-discovery is carried forward by exploring our style of life in light of the demands made upon us and our possibilities for response, and by discovering together the mediums and languages in which we may express who we are and in which we may carry on our mutual ministry.

The experiential process we have proposed is an outgrowth and an expression of Christian ministry, using youth as a paradigm. As such, it could be used by sessions, vestries, deacons, or any group within the church as a way of discovering the common bonds we share by serving Christ in concrete and particular situations. The process will show the interconnectedness of youth ministry with a variety of ministries. Attention to the dynamics of this process will keep leadership training events in the church from focusing on the specialists and ignoring the very people who are engaged in the ministry.

Ways of Following Up the Workshop Experience

The workshop experience can make a difference to the people who have participated. It can be used for youth ministry in the parish. It may be "multiplied" in a number of ways.

The Participants

The heart of the experience has been new insights, new possibilities, and new convictions on the part of those who have been members of the workshop. Ways have been discovered of enriching their experience of Bible study, worship, and personal creative expression. They have been able to reconsider their practice of the Christian life, their faith values, and their relationships.

In addition, they have experienced a new way of putting these matters together. In the experience of these few hours, these elements and emphases have been woven into patterns that hint at wholeness of personal life in a setting of Christian discipleship and social responsibility.

Since all those who have attended have some connection with, or interest in, youth ministry, the experience has been one in which they have seen familiar ideas and experiences reconsidered and enhanced, and new possibilities suggested. Bringing all of these factors together in the context of youth ministry, the participant has perhaps been able to see new roles in a renewed vocation, with youth ministry as a demanding and rewarding calling.

The Parish

The workshop has provided a model for youth ministry in the parish, one that the participants have experienced, become familiar with, and tested. They may be in a position to design similar workshops with youth and youth leaders in the parish itself. If that is not feasible, they may be able to conduct such workshops with youth and youth leaders from their own and neighboring parishes together.

When the workshop is conducted in or for the parish, it is not an end in itself. It serves two purposes:

1. To train youth and adults in leadership for youth ministry.
2. To suggest essential goals, elements, and emphases for youth ministry.

Never an end in itself, the workshop has to be translated back into relationships and programs in the parish, embodying in appropriate ways its goals, its elements, and its emphases.

"Multipliers"

The steering committee can continue to work with the participants. Friendships, personal and professional, have been established, and their multiplying effects cannot be guessed. But in specific ways, the steering committee can help with:

Periodic follow-up correspondence
Reports to sponsoring bodies, with recommendations for their action
Published accounts of the workshop and its aftermath
Recommendations for next steps
Newsletters that share information, experience, and ideas

The participants themselves can multiply the experience by sharing it in formal and informal, planned and unplanned ways with other youth and youth leaders and with other groups.

Chances are that the first workshop experiences will include the more or less usual group of youth leaders. The follow-up may expand that group by reaching out seriously to others for whom it is intended and to whom it would be important and useful. Remember those for whom it is appropriate:

- Youth who are leaders in youth ministry programs
- All adults who work with young persons
  - Assigned leaders
  - Youth ministry administrators
  - Christian education administrators
  - Pastors
  - Support personnel
- Other interested and concerned adults
  - Potential leaders
  - Parents
  - Christian education committee members
  - Church governing council members

Eventually ways may be found for all such persons to share in the workshop experience.

Furthermore, the goals, elements, and emphases that have been tested in this workshop experience may be multiplied as they are experienced and used in:

- Youth curriculum—both nationally produced curriculum, and locally devised curriculum and program.
- The work of various judicatories in program planning resources and resources for leadership development—both professional and volunteer.
- Media for communication among youth and youth leaders—for mutual recognition, mutual support, enabling, and overcoming loneliness; networks of youth, youth leaders, and friends; assemblies; training conferences; groups of interns; additional workshops and clinics; newsletters and periodicals; and other publications.

Bibliography

Don Richter's "A Bibliographical Survey of Youth and Youth Ministry," in *Religious Education Ministry with Youth* (Birmingham, Alabama: Religious Education Press, 1982), analyzed and discussed the most important books on youth and youth ministry, thus putting the essential information in the hands of youth leaders as effectively and economically as possible. Consult that bibliographical essay for basic works on youth ministry theory and adolescent development, as well as for practical guides to teaching and program planning for youth ministry.

Richter's work brings the material up through 1979. The following books have become available since his list was compiled.

Understanding Youth

Adelson, Joseph, ed., *Handbook of Adolescent Psychology*. New York: John Wiley and Sons Inc., 1980.

When the religious educator, in dealing with the question of youth, wants to go beyond popular treatments and surveys of the psychology of adolescents, this handbook will serve well. Summaries of research and theory on key questions of concern to those dealing with youth, written by the most informed persons in the field. Makes reference to the research studies themselves easy.

Brake, Mike, *The Sociology of Youth Culture and Youth Subcultures*. London: Routledge & Kegan Paul Ltd., 1980.

An updating of the sociology of contemporary youth, dealing primarily with the manifestations of youth culture and subcultures in areas of British influence. A chapter, "Dread in Babylon," interprets the Rastafarian phenomenon.

Fowler, James W., *Stages of Faith: the Psychology of Human Development and the Quest for Meaning*. San Francisco: Harper & Row, Publishers, Inc., 1981.

In this long-awaited book, Fowler gives us the mature statement of his research-based "stages of faith development." With the warning that theory must not be limiting, this full presentation of his theory is set in a profoundly challenging psychological and theological context. At the same time it is a personal document in which he discloses his own faith development and invites the reader to do so as well.

Giving Youth a Better Chance: Options for Education, Work and Service. San Francisco: Jossey-Bass Inc., Publishers, 1979.

A substantial study of the "youth problem," concentrating on schooling, employment, and community behavior. Produced by the Carnegie Council on Policy Studies in Higher Education, it provides background materials on the contemporary situation of youth, detailed recommendations, and a useful bibliography.

Hargrove, Barbara, *Religion for a Dislocated Generation*. Valley Forge: Judson Press, 1980.

A study of the faith and religious experience of the youth generation of a decade ago. Both theological and sociological in orientation, it contributes to understanding the psychology of adolescence (and youth adulthood) and the sociology of religion.

Marschak, Marianne, *Parent-Child Interaction and Youth Rebellion*. New York: Gardner Press, Inc., 1980.

A wide-ranging research (international in scope) intended to clarify the nature and meaning of "youth movements." The focus is on the hippie movement in the U.S.A., the German *Wandervogel*, and the Israeli kibbutz, raising the question of why there is radical abandonment of identification with parents. The kibbutz is seen as an example of a youth movement that has been channeled into a reality-based, goal-oriented form of communal life.

Tweddell, Millie, *Parents and Adolescents: The Journey and the Voyage of Life*. New York: Church Education Services, The Program Agency, Presbyterian Church (U.S.A.), 1981.

Christian Education

Bowman, Locke E., Jr., *Teaching Today*. Philadelphia: The Westminster Press, 1980.

A Christian education research specialist, theorist, and trainer, who has done more than anyone else to detail the meaning and dynamics of Christian *teaching*, here sets out his theory in the full context of the church's responsibility. He clarifies learning, teaching, and educational ministry, and brings them into focus.

Dykstra, Craig, *Vision and Character: A Christian Educator's Alternative to Kohlberg*. Ramsey, New Jersey: Paulist Press, 1981.

After a thorough analysis of Kohlberg's "juridical ethics," which he finds not compatible with theological ethics and thus not a direct service to Christian education, Dykstra develops "visional ethics" as an alternative. Its dynamics are imagination and revelation, and its disciplines are repentance, prayer, and service. How the church may appropriate moral education is summed up in the model on page 121.

Groome, Thomas H., *Christian Religion Education: Sharing Our Story and Vision*. San Francisco: Harper & Row, Publishers, Inc., 1980.

Destined to be one of the great books in Christian education, Groome's book presents his "shared praxis" model in fully developed form, and does so in the richest possible context. A critical review of basic theory is informed by comprehensive historical, biblical, theological, philosophical, and educational materials.

Heckman, Shirley J., *On the Wings of a Butterfly: A Guide to Total Christian Education*. Elgin, Illinois: Brethren Press, 1981.

A theory of Christian education, interlaced with much personal experience and many practical illustrations and exercises, developing what it means to be an educating community of faith and action. A good balance is maintained between education into the community and educating for freedom, creativity, and responsibility. This is as close to a whole Christian nurture as any contemporary Christian education theorist has come.

Youth Ministry

Adebonojo, Mary, *Free to Choose*. Youth Program Resource from the Black Experience. Valley Forge: Judson Press, 1980.

Benson, Dennis C., and Wolfe, Bill, *The Basic Encyclopedia for Youth Ministry*. Loveland, Colorado: Group Books, 1981.

A book for dipping in where and when you need it. Short, helpful articles on everything from bell choirs to "X-rated," curriculum to "T.A.," dieting to Sunday church school. A topical guide gives the major themes: adults and youth ministry, interpersonal, media, when the going gets tough, youth culture, the basics, creative ministry, youth group management, and youth group problems. Many articles are cross-referenced to other related subjects, and there are citations to additional resources.

Hargrove, Barbara, and Jones, Stephen D., *Reaching Youth Today: Heirs to the Whirlwind*. Valley Forge: Judson Press, 1983.

Barbara Hargrove, a sociologist of religion, places today's youth in the context of a dynamic youth culture with specific roots and definite stages of historical development. She relates that youth culture to the world of work, to self-identity, and to public responsibility. Stephen Jones, pastor, faces the question of evangelism—"reaching" these youth, nurturing them, enabling them to experience conversion, and relating that evangelism to the realities of their culture.

Harris, Maria, *Portrait of Youth Ministry*. Ramsey, New Jersey: Paulist Press, 1981.

Maria Harris has a way of identifying important issues in a new way, burrowing into them with new intent, and coming up with suggestions that represent new insight. In this book she and her students have done this for the field of youth ministry in a way that conveys excitement and practical guidance.

Holderness, Ginny Ward, *Youth Ministry: The New Team Approach*. Atlanta, Georgia: John Knox Press, 1981.

Jones, Jeffrey D., and Potts, Kenneth C., *Organizing a Youth Ministry to Fit Your Needs*. Valley Forge: Judson Press, 1983.

The authors identify three approaches to youth ministry, centered on meetings, events, or individuals. Guidance is given in determining which approach is best in a particular situation and how it may be developed to meet the needs of the situation.

David Ng, *Youth in the Community of Disciples*. Valley Forge: Judson Press, 1984.

The author calls for churches to emphasize the call to discipleship through the ministry of the church, in the place of "fun and games" for youth.

Stone, J. David, ed., *The Complete Youth Ministries Handbook, Volume One*. Nashville: Abingdon Press, 1979.

Leadership

Hayes, Rebecca S., *Youth Developing a Church Training Group*. Nashville: Convention Press, 1981.

McKinley, John, *Group Development through Participation Training*. Ramsey, New Jersey: Paulist Press, 1980.

A manual for the development of membership skills for effective group work, geared to the church situation. A "Participant's Manual" accompanies the "Trainer's Resource."

Richards, Lawrence O., and Hoeldtke, Clyde, *A Theology of Church Leadership*. Grand Rapids, Michigan: Zondervan Publishing House, 1980.

Manages in a fruitful way to provide a thoroughgoing and critical treatment of what is known about leadership from organizational management and social psychological points of view, but within a rich and consistent theological framework that makes that information useful to the church in authentic ways. Clarifies the nature of ministry, broadly understood, within the context of church renewal.

Rusbuldt, Richard E., *Basic Teacher Skills, Handbook for Church School Teachers*. Valley Forge: Judson Press, 1981.

A very personal and graphic orientation to the task of teaching. The teacher's roles are clarified, and a systematic step-by-step plan for getting ready to teach is laid out and illustrated by citing and explaining a variety of teaching activities and their uses. Substantive attention is given to the questions that come up in the volunteer teacher's career. A leader's guide is included in the book.

Bible Study

Metcalf, William, *Sixteen Methods of Group Bible Study*, Valley Forge: Judson Press, 1980.

Orr, Dick and Bartlett, David L., *Bible Journeys: Experiences for Christian Growth*. A Youth Resource. Valley Forge: Judson Press, 1980.

Wink, Walter, *Transforming Bible Study, A Leader's Guide*. Nashville: Abingdon Press, 1980.

Building on his previous book, *The Bible in Human Transformation*, the author here becomes much more explicit about the methods and materials for his approach to Bible study. A treatment of the underlying theory is followed by an overview of the method. The rest of the book consists of explanatory and illustrative detail.

Weber, Hans-Ruedi, *Experiments with Bible Study*. Geneva: World Council of Churches, 1981.

Weber writes, "Listening, analyzing, and reading, students of the Bible meet a living reality which begins to challenge them. . . . This divine presence starts to question, judge, and guide us. Perhaps gradually, perhaps quite suddenly, the book which was the object of our reading and study becomes a subject which reads us." Part I discusses the bases for such Bible study and the ways it may be conducted. Part II consists of twenty-five accounts of such Bible study experiences.

Expressive Activities

Wolterstorff, Nicholas, *Art in Action*. Grand Rapids, Michigan: Wm. B. Eerdmanns Publishing Company, 1980.

The growing literature on art and religion finds a valuable addition in this book on aesthetic theory by a Christian philosopher who says, "Works of art are objects and instruments of action. They are all inextricably embedded in the fabric of human intention. They are objects and instruments of action whereby we carry out our intentions with respect to the world, our fellows, ourselves, and our gods." Some rather specific clues for Christian education are found in the final section, "Participation."

Youth Ministry and the Christian Life

Brister, C. W., *Becoming You: A Young Person's Guide for Living*. Nashville: Broadman Press, 1980.

LeFever, Marlene D., *Toward Freedom, A Teacher's Guide to Helping Teens*. Elgin, Illinois: David C. Cook Publishing Company, 1979.

Owens, Owen D., *Growing Churches for a New Age*. Valley Forge: Judson Press, 1981.

Detailed case studies of churches that have defined or redefined themselves as visionary, incarnational, witnessing, relational, and activist. "New life broke into these congregations out of a shattering or dissolving of what they have been."

Wolterstorff, Nicholas P., *Education for Responsible Action*. Grand Rapids, Michigan: Wm. B. Eerdmans Publishing Company, 1980.

A provocative and helpful discussion of what the author calls "tendency learning," that is, learning that results in tendencies to act. Some religious educators would refer to it as an "ethical action" approach. Against the background of rival educational theories, the case is made for discipline and modeling as appropriate dynamics, coupled with internalization. A major treatment of a significant aspect of a Christian philosophy of education.

Faith Values in Youth Ministry

Jones, Stephen D., *Faith Shaping: Nurturing the Faith Journey of Youth*. Valley Forge: Judson Press, 1980.

A popular but profound treatment of growth in faith in adolescence. Realistic about social change, the author insists that the nurture of youth in faith must today be very consciously intentional. A wealth of practical suggestions is backed up by theological and psychological understandings. Most valuable is the clarification of adult roles in the process.

Rice, F. Philip, *Morality and Youth: A Guide for Christian Parents*. Philadelphia: The Westminster Press, 1980.

Presents a comprehensive scheme for moral education, rooted in research and theory in moral development, and reflecting specific Christian values. The area is defined and delineated, methods and contexts (religious education being one) are discussed, and specific problem areas are addressed.

Westley, Dick, *Redemptive Intimacy: A New Perspective for the Journey to Adult Faith*. Mystic, Connecticut: Twenty-Third Publications Inc., 1981.

Distinguishing between faith and religion, the author convincingly suggests an experiential and dialogical approach to growth in faith that has its focus in what he calls redemptive intimacy, a human experience that is founded on God's redemptive presence, sought and acknowledged. An appropriate context for him is the "household church."

Wingeier, Douglas E., *Working Out Your Own Beliefs: A Guide for Doing Your Own Theology*. Nashville: Abingdon Press, 1980.

The author takes the four approaches to religious truth that are characteristic of the United Methodist Church—experience, reason, Scripture, and tradition—and shows how each may be implemented in specific ways by persons concerned with deepening their theological understandings and their faith.

Relational Factors in Youth Ministry

Richards, Lawrence O., and Martin, Gib, *A Theology of Personal Ministry*. Grand Rapids, Michigan: The Zondervan Corp., 1981.

Richards and Martin work essentially from a covenant concept of the church to an identification of particular gifts in ministry, conceiving ministry as a basically lay function in which clergy share. Theological and biblical analyses and imperatives undergird the argument, and what the authors call "probes" provide illustrative material and enable the readers to arrive at their own particular implication.

Russell, Letty M., *Growth in Partnership*. Philadelphia: The Westminster Press, 1981.

Russell here comes back to the specific theme of educational ministry, developed around the concept of partnership. There is a developing community of learning that aims toward both "building the Body" and "growth toward maturity," through partnership. This is tied to liberation themes as "education as exodus" and "pedagogy for oppressors" are explored. A pervasive concern is a new approach to theological education.

Afterword

D. Campbell Wyckoff

I am taking the privilege of adding a personal "afterword" to this manual. Sara Little was appointed by the Lilly Endowment, Inc., as evaluator for our project, and sent each of the participants a set of four questions on which to comment. The questions, and my own personal comments, are as follows:

1. Did the workshop accomplish the goal set for it? Why or why not?

   The thing that impressed me most about the goal of the workshop was the fact that it was wholeheartedly accepted by all of the participants. I have never been a part of an event in which those involved worked so creatively and constructively together to accomplish the purpose set. The wide variety of backgrounds, talents, and professional approaches and experience were offered in the most open way to the group as it explored and formed its design for youth ministry.

2. Analyzing your own experience in the workshop, what did you find to be of greater or lesser value?

   There were two elements that I felt had to be included in the workshop—first, the examination and enrichment of our own approaches to youth ministry, and second, the careful analysis and critique of that experience. There is no question but that the first was accomplished in the most thoroughgoing and exciting way. The group was, perhaps, a bit reluctant to shift gears at the appropriate point in the schedule to the second element (this came to light in a meeting of the steering committee). But it was persuaded to do so and the results were superb. As a symbol of this, there was some pressure to move the closing worship to an earlier time. This was protested on the grounds that that experience should catch up both the experiential and the analytical and critical elements of the workshop. That view prevailed and the workshop remained a unit.

3. What in your judgment is the distinctive contribution that might be anticipated from the design emerging from the workshop?

   A thoroughly worked out way of helping persons in youth ministry to explore their own identities and to direct their new understandings toward the various elements and functions of ministry with youth.

   Identification of the elements and emphases essential to youth ministry, and clarification of the ways in which those elements and emphases form a functional unity.

   Clarity as to the dynamics working in the training process of ministers with youth.

4. What other personal reflections do you have on the workshop?

   It was such an ambitious project that I went into it with some real misgivings. It turned out to be very exciting, enriching, and, in a tremendously vital way, disturbing. I have been working it through in various ways ever since!

My experiences, feelings, and hopes are best caught up, however, in the letter that I wrote to the members of the experimental workshop when it was over. I hope that those going through the experience described in this manual may be able to echo such sentiments!

Dear Steve, Bill, Freda, Marlene, Dave, Jean, Wayne, Don, Manford, Bob, and Roger,

The more I have thought about it, the more it has

seemed to me that a "general" note of appreciation would be the appropriate way to thank all of you who were in the Youth Ministry Workshop last week. I personally have seldom had such a rich and moving experience of unity in Christ, or of a group working through a demanding task so creatively and productively, and in such a spirit.

Since returning here, those of us in Princeton have shared our observations on how remarkably the elements of careful planning, competent and sensitive leadership, and resourceful participation blended in the event, and how the critical analysis and reconstructive thought of the last day emerged from and were strengthened by the experiences we had together in the first three days.

If what we experienced can be caught in some authentic way and rendered communicable to others, we will have gone well beyond my own original hopes for the project. This is the task immediately ahead.

My deep sense of gratitude to all of you reflects the fact of having received a profoundly important gift of grace through you in our work together.

Very sincerely,

Cam